Better Homes and Gardens.

Easiest Plants

You Can Grow

**BETTER HOMES AND
GARDENS BOOKS**

Editor: Gerald Knox
Art Director:
  Ernest Shelton
Associate Art Director:
  Randall Yontz
Production and
Copy Editors:
  Paul S. Kitzke
  David Kirchner
Garden and Outdoor
Living Editor:
  Beverly Garrett
Garden Book Editor:
  Marjorie P. Groves
Senior Garden Editor:
  Russell O'Harra
Easiest Plants You Can Grow
  Editor: Kay Stroud
Senior Graphic Designer:
  Harijs Priekulis
Graphic Designers:
  Faith Berven
  Sheryl Veenschoten
  Richard Lewis
  Neoma Alt West
  Linda Ford

CONTENTS

A Guide for Low-care Gardens

Smart Uses for Easy Plants

There are a few tricks to every trade, and gardening is no exception. It's easy to grow orchids in jungles. It's also easy to grow cacti in a desert. Easy gardening depends on matching the right plant with the right place. Choose the correct plant for a given spot, and half the battle's won. This book is designed to help you do just that. In a shady retreat, above, container gardening is smart gardening. Ferns, ivy, blue lobelia, caladium, and impatiens thrive.

Smart Uses for Easy Plants

For easy care of any garden, whether it is as small as a planting pocket or as large as your imagination can make it, the secret lies in selecting the right plants for the right spot.

It's wise to choose a few perennial plants—trees, shrubs, evergreens—because they supply permanent greenery and a variety of textures.

For easy color, rely on bedding plants massed in one area for major effect, and have container-grown flowering plants that can be replaced as their blooming season ends.

In the narrow space at the side of the house pictured here, all these rules have been followed. A graceful Japanese maple, with glossy boxwood in a plant box behind it and feathery ferns opposite, are permanent parts of the landscape.

Blooming plants and color come from the massed planting at the foot of the maple. These include fibrous begonias that will go on blooming all summer and pots of cyclamen sunk into the ground.

For early color here, the spring pink of container-grown azaleas is placed in strategic spots. When their season of bloom ends, they could well be replaced by container-grown caladiums or tuberous begonias.

Notice that everything you see in this garden, as well as the replacements suggested, are all plants that tolerate or do best in shade. Were this a sunny area, the same goal of easy care could be achieved by selecting different plants: pots of geraniums instead of azaleas, a flowering shrub such as hibiscus in place of the ferns, petunias instead of ever-blooming begonias. These are only a few of the good alternate choices you could make and still have minimal care.

Another factor to consider is the region you live in. Obviously, the garden pictured is in an area where winters are mild. In sections where winters are long and temperatures are frequently below freezing, your selection of plants would be different.

Your choice of planters is important, too. A hodgepodge of different sizes, styles, and colors can destroy the pleasing effect you want. Natural wood containers and terra-cotta pots look good together and are always safe to combine. All-white containers look great on many patios, as do shades of brown or black.

It is the major goal of this book to help you select the plants—trees, shrubs, vines, flowering perennials, bulbs, ground covers, wildflowers, herbs, and bulbs—that are easy to grow.

Start by consulting the zone map on page 94, if you do not already know the growing region in which you live. Use it as a guide in the selection of plants that thrive in your kind of climate.

For additional ideas on all types of plants, seek advice at your county or state extension service. You'll be able to find pamphlets containing information on landscape and ornamental plants recommended for your area, including rate of growth—slow, medium, rapid—as well as height at maturity.

If there is one near your home, visit an arboretum so you can see many kinds of trees. Visit large nurseries carrying a variety of trees and shrubs to help decide on the ones you like best. Drive around your town or city and look at the trees in residential areas to see how various trees look at maturity—they will be very unlike the slender saplings you may plant.

Depending on the size of your property, seek a variety of sizes and textures in the trees and shrubs you plant. If the area is small, don't try to squeeze in one of everything. Allow for growth, even though plants are very small when they're planted.

If possible, try to include evergreen and deciduous trees and shrubs. They complement each other in both shape and texture, and, in colder climates, you'll still have something green to look at all winter.

These suggestions are not only for those planning a new garden; the points are also applicable if you already have many plants on your lot but are not happy about the amount of time you spend caring for them. Use our tips to help decide what to eliminate and how to select replacements that demand less of you.

Choosing Entry Plantings

Better than a welcome mat are well-chosen plants and trees that lead visitors to the entrance of your home. Plantings may be formal or informal, depending on your home's style of architecture and your personal tastes. The beauty of your home depends greatly on the plantings around it, so don't neglect this important feature. Just a few plants can make a surprising difference. Think first of low maintenance and year-round beauty when choosing plants.

If trees and shrubs are prominent parts of your plan, choose them first. If you live in a cold region of the country, needled evergreens should receive top billing, though they may be mixed with deciduous plants that retain attractive outlines even without foliage in winter months.

Consider the price of major landscape plantings as an investment, not an expense. Trees and shrubs grow in value as they grow in size. You'll enjoy their beauty and the increased property value they'll help to bring about.

When planting any shrubs or trees, carefully consider their placement, taking into account mature height and breadth. For example, we all have seen gorgeous spruces that as small specimen plants were planted on both sides of an entrance; as mature plants, however, they crowd awkwardly against house and entryway, no longer in scale with their surroundings. With older landscapes, it is often best to cut out problem plants and start over.

Next to trees and shrubs in importance are ground covers. Choose those that will remain evergreen for most of the year in cold climates or throughout the year if you live where winters are mild.

For every tree, shrub, ground cover, or flowering plant you include in your design, keep in mind the amount of sun or shade each plant requires. Choose those that will prosper using the sunlight falling in your entryway.

Some of the shrubs and trees you select for entry plantings may flower at certain seasons of the year; some may have berries or fruit of bright color that stay in place for many months. Make sure colors blend with those of your house and with any flowering plants you set in place as seasonal accents.

Pocket plantings of pansies, violas, or spring-flowering bulbs can make cheerful, colorful additions to entry plantings. But remember they will not stay in bloom for very long, and in the case of bulbs whose foliage must be allowed to ripen and fall off, be prepared to lift and replant them elsewhere once blooms fade.

One way to do this easily is to grow them in pots sunk into the ground. Simply lift and replace them with other flowering plants whose bloom will continue through the summer months or with such plants as chrysanthemums, which will not begin to bloom until early fall.

This technique, known as plunge gardening, is used widely in large public gardens where color is wanted, with bloom in peak condition during an entire growing season.

Another factor to keep in mind as you plan entry plantings is good variety of color and texture. Shiny leaves look even shinier contrasted with fuzzy or needled foliage. And remember there are many shades of green, ranging from the nearly blue tones to darkest green.

Well-placed rocks and low-growing succulents match architecture of house.

An enclosed entry garden may feature an array of plants, such as the liriope, Boston ivy, and geraniums used here.

Pocket Plantings

If you plan to remodel the entrance to your home or to install a patio, consider including some planting pockets in areas otherwise surfaced with stone or concrete aggregate. A glance at the illustrations on these pages will show you the impact of even very small planting areas.

Don't let expense limit you. A few packets of seed can add important color. Or, if time's the thing, a few flats of bedding plants can do the trick for a modest sum. If you have no planting pockets, consider filling some large pots or planters to set in strategic spots. But if you do it this way to get splashes of color, be prepared to water regularly. Container-grown plants can be half cooked by blazing sun, particularly if they're placed on a paved surface or next to a wall that reflects heat.

A wide range of annuals, such as marigold, petunia, alyssum, ageratum, and nasturtium are naturals if there is adequate sunshine (at least four hours per day, preferably six). But there are also colorful, shade-loving plants. Caladiums (grown from tubers) are a favorite, as are tuberous begonias. These tubers can be lifted before the first frost, stored in a cool, dry place over winter, and re-grown the following year. For an early start, they should be planted indoors four to six weeks before the last expected freeze, then transplanted to their outdoor location for color and bloom the entire summer season.

Spring-flowering bulbs, such as the species tulips, scillas, snowdrops, hyacinths, and daffodils, are good subjects for pocket plantings. Plan to overplant these spring beauties later with plants that will hide the foliage of the bulbs as it yellows and ripens—a must if you expect the bulbs to bloom again the following spring. Or dig the bulbs up and replant elsewhere after their season of bloom has ended.

An ornamental tree included in the planting pocket—such as saucer magnolia, redbud, and some of the flowering crabs—makes a hand-some addition to your landscaping plan. But be sure to water it well during dry weather, because most of its roots are covered with a hard surface, limiting its access to rainfall.

If your patio is too sunny, plant a tree like the one at right that will also cast welcome shade. The locust is a good choice; redbud, crabapple, and saucer magnolia give seasonal flowers as well as shade.

A root waterer attached to a garden hose and thrust deep into the ground near the tree works well here. Left running at a slow rate for a long period, it is one way to get water to tree roots. Another is using a soaker hose.

For a planting pocket with a tree as its central element, the surface of the ground around it may be planted with colorful blooming plants (see photographs on this page).

For even lower maintenance, use a perennial ground cover (vinca, ajuga) or one of the succulents ("hen and chicks," for example). Or simply cover exposed ground with attractive pebbles or crushed rock that offer a colorful contrast to surrounding paved surfaces. This requires nothing more than pulling out an occasional weed that may grow through the layer of pebbles or rocks.

This retainer island is edged by redwood 2x4s. The inner one holds coarse rock chips; the outer is planted with easy-to-grow white and purple alyssum, dwarf marigolds.

When azalea blossoms fade, ageratum and campanulas fill the area with bloom.

This mixed border includes Blue Blazer ageratum, Astro (red-white) petunias, and Maytime (salmon-pink grandiflora) petunias.

Planting Plans for Low-care Gardens

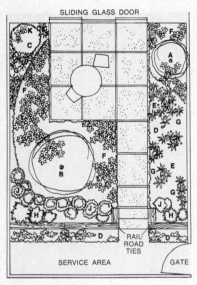

SLIDING GLASS DOOR

SERVICE AREA

RAIL ROAD TIES

GATE

A Dogwood
B Willow Oak
C Rhododendron
D Bedding plants
E Daffodil
F Ivy
G Tulip
H Firs
J Azalea
K Wisteria

Dining al fresco *is one of the amenities a well-planned townhouse garden provides.*

Townhouses and condominiums in urban areas usually have space behind each housing unit for a patio garden. Sizes and shapes of plants are especially important when space is limited.

Many, if not most, residents in such developments are people who don't want to do much gardening but still want a touch of the gracious life a small, private garden can provide.

Successful planting in this setting depends largely on scale. As in a terrarium where a table palm seems impressively tall in relation to tiny plants nearby, so in the garden pictured above, a willow oak, with its light network of leaves that lets sunlight filter through, seems larger than its actual size.

Consult the list at left to see how the rest of the plantings have been chosen and placed. Notice that each of the azaleas is spaced so the entire plant shows to advantage.

The flower show begins in spring with massed daffodils. Then azaleas, rhododendron, and a carpet of tulips take over, with flowering dogwood adding color at a higher level.

During the summer, wisteria, trained to frame the living room window, begins to bloom. Zinnias, marigolds, and petunias thrive in the sunniest areas of planting beds; impatiens and fibrous begonias splash color in shadier spots. The lush carpet of ivy ties the various planting areas together visually and, unlike grass, requires no mowing.

A small pool and fountain make this shaded garden an inviting summer room.

A Andromeda
B Scarlet oak
C Azalea
D Pyracantha
E Japanese holly
G Rhododendron
H Climbing rose Don Juan

This townhouse garden, like the one pictured opposite, is located in Baltimore where summers are warm. A small, shady garden is a pleasant, outdoor oasis. Beneath the windows, a small pool with splashing fountain enhances the "cool" feeling this well-designed garden offers. The pool's location in the sunniest part of the garden allows the growing of waterlilies and other aquatics.

With a submersible pump recirculating the water, a fountain can be featured in any garden. A bridge over the pool, fashioned from 2x4 strips of stained redwood, link house and patio paved in bluestone.

By practicing vertical gardening, the owner manages to have many blooming plants, even though he has covered most of the area with flagstone. Climbing roses and pyracantha grow up, not out, and so save space.

The key tree in the plan at right is a scarlet oak that provides shade all summer and color in the fall. It also provides the filtered light essential to keep the azaleas healthy. Under its protective branches, dining among colorful plants is a pleasure.

Before you plant anything in a small-scale garden, shop around for small varieties of plants that won't quickly outgrow the space you've allotted or require frequent, time-consuming pruning. Because they're easy to maintain, the time you spend this way will pay off handsomely in years to come.

ANNUALS

For Carefree Color

If you plan to start your first flower garden but don't have much time to take care of it, look to the colorful and inexpensive annuals. Though eventually you may intend to have a great border of mixed perennials, you'll still find annuals to be your very best friends when you begin. Perennials usually take at least two years—more often three—before their bloom is generous. But you don't want to wait two or three years for colorful bloom. You want it now! And have it you will, if you plant annuals from seed or started seedlings. The mass of annual candytuft in the bed pictured at right is bordered with vivid pink pelargoniums. If you begin with flats of candytuft and small pots of pelargoniums ready to bloom, you can duplicate this scene in weeks. Both plants are tender and can't take frost, but if you set them into a well-prepared, sunny bed as soon as the soil has warmed and the last freeze has passed, you can sit back and wait—not long— for a picture like this in your very first flower garden. Exciting? Yes, annuals are exciting and easy-to-grow plants every gardener should enjoy.

Annuals for Sunny Spots

It's difficult to beat some of the favorite annuals for quick color and easy maintenance. Pictured, *below*, is an example of what you can do to get a dash of color at the edge of a deck. Combined are Scarlet Ruffles zinnias and Yellow Nugget Marigolds.

Scarlet Ruffles puts up sturdy 28-inch stems; great for bouquets. Yellow Nugget begins blooming just five weeks after you sow the seed.

Nugget Marigolds bloom all summer.

For bloom that just won't stop, rely on annuals in beds or borders where they can get ample sun. There are, of course, a number of annuals that do well in full or partial shade, but most heavy-blooming types need nearly full sun.

Of course, you can save money if you grow your plants from seed. And you can also get just the variety you want, one you may not be able to find if you buy bedding plants at nurseries. But some annuals with extra-fine seed or long germination periods probably should be bought as bedding plants when the weather is warm enough to set them out. Petunias and alyssum are two favorites that fall into this group—they're somewhat difficult for amateurs to grow from seed.

Among the hardy annuals that are easy to grow from seed sown out of doors as soon as soil can be worked are: California poppy, candytuft, bachelor's button, four o'clocks, pinks, evening-primrose, larkspur, snapdragon, moss rose, and snow-on-the mountain.

For later planting—after the soil has warmed—are these annuals: balsam, cleome, cockscomb, dusty miller, godetia, gypsoyphila, marigold, nasturtium, nicotiana, statice, sunflower, and zinnia.

If you decide to buy bedding plants, you'll find that nurseries offer them for sale in flats. Buy a full flat, or buy "ponies"—plants by the dozen. Or you can buy small plastic trays containing six or eight plants.

However you buy bedding plants, be sure they are bushy. If they have been pinched back earlier, they will not be leggy and will have many side branches along their stems.

Whether you plant seeds or young bedding plants, it's important to prepare new beds in advance—the previous fall, if possible. To ensure success, soil samples from various parts of your garden should be analyzed. Afterward, add any missing elements to the soil.

When planning flower borders, keep in mind the ultimate heights and widths of the annuals you are combining. Aim for a gradual rise in heights from the low edging plants to the tall plants at the rear of the bed. And don't scatter individual plants throughout the border. Instead, arrange irregular patches of a dozen or more identical plants to get bold splashes of color.

Crowding plants can decrease their vigor and flower production, so space most annuals eight to 12 inches apart. If your soil is beautifully prepared and enriched, you can space plants even farther apart. If planting seed, space the seeds at least half an inch apart for easy thinning later on.

One of the tricks that make gardening easy is growing flowering plants in big tubs, pots, boxes—even barrels, for vining annuals—to get vivid color that can be moved where you want it. Successful container gardening makes it possible to have color on or near the patio, the sun deck, the balcony, at your front entry—wherever it might be difficult to get the seasonal color you want in any other way.

This method also lets you have a changing scene to match the sea-

sons. You might start with pots of pansies or violas in spring, followed, when these are no longer in peak condition, by bush-form sweet peas, then geraniums—or a mixture of sun-loving annuals—that will carry on all summer long. Remove spent blooms to encourage constant summer bloom.

Container gardening differs from the usual method of setting plants into soil. First, you'll need to check

water needs frequently, daily in hot or windy weather. Because it is more exposed, soil in containers dries out from evaporation more rapidly than soil in garden beds.

Second, be careful not to place container gardens on concrete or other hard-surfaced areas that get full sun all day. The reflected heat will be too much for almost any plant. For the same reason, don't set containers next to heat-reflecting walls.

Finally, be sure to provide adequate drainage. If you set a clay pot into a decorated container with no drainage holes after each watering, make sure the pots are not sitting in water. This is also important if container-grown plants inside decorative cover-ups are left outdoors during a rain. Plant roots will rot quickly if the pots stand in water for any length of time.

The raised planter, *above,* borders a deck with joyous color combinations and generous bloom. You can get this effect only by combining a number of annuals. Included are pinks, lobelia, dwarf marigolds, petunias in several hues, and sweet smelling alyssum. In the background, the feathery green foliage of cosmos adds texture and height. For more information on annuals, see the "ABCs" section on pages 62 to 64.

17

For Sunny Beds

Topper snapdragons, in mixed colors, offer a steady supply of flower spires. Snapdragons come easily from seed and are good for cutting as well.

Few annuals make hedges, but tall-growing salvia can serve as a property divider.

In addition to the snapdragon, salvia, and rudbeckia pictured on these pages, other easy-to-grow annuals include sweet alyssum, annual aster, California poppy, annual candytuft, cockscomb, cosmos, bachelor's button, phlox, nasturtium, scabiosa, and zinnia in many sizes and colors.

All have long seasons of bloom, providing you keep spent blooms cut. All are good candidates for colorful indoor bouquets.

By choosing from the many kinds of annuals and their varieties, you can plant entire beds or borders. Plant tall-growing kinds to the rear of the border, those of medium height (ten to 14 inches) in mid-border locations, and low-growing or dwarf varieties along the front edge. For additional help on planning a sunny border, see the sun-loving perennials on pages 24 and 25.

If you plan to grow most of your annuals from seed, check the information on seed packets to learn the length of germination. That way, you'll be able to determine when seed should be started before young plants can be set into the garden. The average period for sowing seed in a greenhouse or indoors is six to ten weeks before the last expected freeze in your section of the country.

Many annuals are hardy and can be sown outdoors as soon as the danger of a heavy frost has passed.

In warm areas, these same annuals may be sown outdoors in late fall and early winter. The group includes alyssum, bells of Ireland, calendula, annual candytuft, clarkia, cleome, cosmos, bachelor's button, gaillardia, gloriosa daisy, larkspur, nigella, Shirley and California poppies, salpiglossis, scabiosa, statice, and sweet sultan.

Although the temptation to include some of everything is great, it's not the best way to get truly dramatic results. Using only one variety in a small bed, or two at most, with the second as an edging, is very pleasing.

For large borders, plant large patches of each variety of annual plants you choose. This will give you sweeps of a single color, rather than the spotty effect you get from scattering single plants in the border.

Look for brilliantly colorful twosomes, such as Primrose Lady Hybrid marigold—an All-America Winner—in deep orange color with large blooms that grow as tall as 20 inches, combined with Red Cascade grandiflora petunia in front of the planting. This newer petunia, a fiery red, has big bloom and can grow as tall as 14 inches.

Cascade petunias also lend themselves to hanging basket and window box plantings. Both will bloom from early summer to the first killing frost. For a less flamboyant combination, try Giant Hyacinth-flowered Iceberg candytuft (14 inches tall), bordered by either Rosie O'Day or Carpet of Snow sweet alyssum. Both grow to about four inches tall and will stay in bloom from early summer to fall.

A clump of rudbeckia Marmalade will cheer you all summer. Only 22 inches tall, it's the best one of the annuals for bedding.

For Shady Spots

Most of the free-flowering plants among the annuals require full or nearly full sun; still, a surprising number tolerate shade quite well and provide color in shady spots.

One of the best known and most easily cared for is the large family of impatiens plants—sometimes called, oddly, patience plants. In the last decade, a number of hybrids have been developed, so you can now choose from a wider range of colors, heights, and kinds of foliage.

As a result of hybridizing, you can obtain both seed and started impatiens plants, from six-inch dwarfs to two-foot specimens—the latter are usually available from seed only as mixed colors.

Other dwarf varieties include the mixed Elfin hybrids that grow from seed in a range of white, pink, red, and purple and are six to eight inches at maturity. Huckabuc, in the same group, has an unusually large bloom—as much as 1¾ inches wide—in bicolor orchid and white.

If orange is one of your favorite flower colors, you'll like Tangerine, with abundant flowers all summer on sturdy 15-inch plants.

One of the smaller varieties, hybrid Twinkles, begins its blooming season early, with flowers that include bicolors of fuchsia, red, scarlet, each mixed with white. Plants are dwarf and are good edgers.

If you're starting from seed, sow indoors about eight to ten weeks before the last expected freeze. When transplanting to an outdoor location, set plants about a foot apart. If you take cuttings as soon as the cool nights settle in, you can have blooming pot plants indoors all winter long. Cut four-inch slips and root in well-moistened sand or vermiculite. They'll also root in water; but the roots will be brittle, and you must be careful when moving rooted cuttings to potting soil. *Note of caution:* if you wait too long to take cuttings, plants will have begun to "harden off," and it may be impossible to get them to put out roots.

Other colorful annuals for mostly shaded areas include ageratum, wax begonia, coleus, nicotiana, pansy, and torenia (wishbone plant). Sweet alyssum, although it blooms best in full sun, also does well in partly shaded spots and areas where it receives only morning sun.

One of the plants grown for foliage rather than bloom is coleus. It enjoys morning sun, but it grows well in otherwise shaded areas. In fact, coleus colors are stronger when grown in shade. Bright sun will bleach the bright leaves, or even burn them.

Annuals that provide easy color in shade are great to combine with perennials suited to partial shade. Many of these—daylilies, astilbe, heuchera, and perennial forms of rudbeckia—do not bloom until mid- or late summer. By setting out flower-

Here's an excellent example of the abundant color you get from a bed planted solely with impatiens and set in a shaded area.

ing annuals in a bed of mixed perennials, you get color in shade much earlier than you would if you relied only on the perennials.

Other shade-loving perennials that combine effectively with the annuals described here are the members of the hosta tribe. It's a large family and one that seems to keep growing every year. Hostas do bloom—mostly in July and August—but are grown primarily for their interesting and widely varied foliage. There are hosta varieties for every section of the border. Some varieties grow just four inches tall for a most unusual border—others range in height from eight inches to three feet. The photograph on page 27 illustrates just how well hostas, impatiens, and fibrous begonias give you color in shade.

Container plantings of the annuals mentioned are another way to get color in shady areas. Big pots of almost any of the plants listed among annuals for shade make handsome spots of color on a patio that gets only morning sun—or on a balcony, if you're an apartment dweller. Remember, though, that all container-grown plants need to be watered often. In warm and windy weather, pots may have to be watered daily, because more moisture is evaporated compared with garden beds.

Be sure to provide for adequate drainage. If you set a clay pot inside a more decorative container, check after each rain to make sure the pot is not sitting in the overflow of rainwater. If the water is not emptied within a short time, the plant will die.

Although fibrous or wax begonias are excellent candidates for shady locations, it's probably wise to purchase them as bedding plants, unless you can use a greenhouse to start them from seed. If you do grow them indoors, sow the seed in January or February so you can set them out in spring. These begonias will grow bigger and bloom better if grown where they get either early morning or late evening sun. Growth is a little spindly if plants are in the shade all day long.

You can, however, cut expenses for following seasons if you buy bedding plants the first year. Take four-inch cuttings in late summer and root in moist vermiculite. Pot and set it in a sunny window.

Grow coleus as a container plant in shade—in green and white or green with reds.

Planted to alyssum and fibrous begonias, this lightly shaded path says, "Welcome."

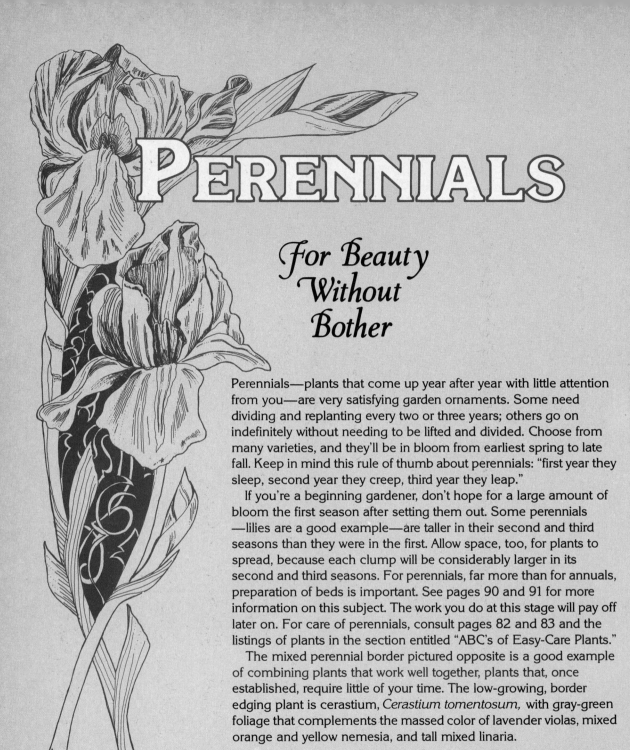

PERENNIALS

For Beauty Without Bother

Perennials—plants that come up year after year with little attention from you—are very satisfying garden ornaments. Some need dividing and replanting every two or three years; others go on indefinitely without needing to be lifted and divided. Choose from many varieties, and they'll be in bloom from earliest spring to late fall. Keep in mind this rule of thumb about perennials: "first year they sleep, second year they creep, third year they leap."

If you're a beginning gardener, don't hope for a large amount of bloom the first season after setting them out. Some perennials —lilies are a good example—are taller in their second and third seasons than they were in the first. Allow space, too, for plants to spread, because each clump will be considerably larger in its second and third seasons. For perennials, far more than for annuals, preparation of beds is important. See pages 90 and 91 for more information on this subject. The work you do at this stage will pay off later on. For care of perennials, consult pages 82 and 83 and the listings of plants in the section entitled "ABC's of Easy-Care Plants."

The mixed perennial border pictured opposite is a good example of combining plants that work well together, plants that, once established, require little of your time. The low-growing, border edging plant is cerastium, *Cerastium tomentosum,* with gray-green foliage that complements the massed color of lavender violas, mixed orange and yellow nemesia, and tall mixed linaria.

For Sunny Beds

Forever is a very long time, and few perennials can claim such great longevity. But the peony and the daylily come very close. A clump of peonies in rich soil can stay in place, increasing in size year after year. Mercy, the variety pictured, *left,* is one of the classic single peony group.

Daylilies are also easily cared for. They, too, can put out satisfactory bloom and can do so even in partial shade with no yearly attention from you. Neither of these plants puts forth a large amount of bloom the first year after planting, but thereafter each supplies plenty for both the garden and cutting.

Both come in a tremendous range of varieties. You can have early, late, or mid-season varieties of each. Heights, too, vary widely.

These two perennials, plus the fall-blooming chrysanthemums, are best known by most perennial lovers, though chrysanthemums are not quite so carefree as their spring and

---

CHOOSE PERENNIALS BY HEIGHT

Front-of-the-Border *(Dwarf to 15 inches)*	Mid-Border *(15 to 30 inches)*	Back-of-the-Border *(over 30 inches)*
Aster (dwarf Michaelmas varieties)	Allium (bulb)	Anchusa (variety Dropmore)
Baby's breath (*Gypsophila repens*)	Balloon flower (platycodon)	Aster, hardy (Michaelmas daisies)
Bellflower (*Campanula carpatica*)	Beebalm (monarda)	Baptisia (false indigo)
Bugloss (anchusa)	Butterfly weed (*Asclepias tuberosa*)	Coneflower (rudbeckia)
Candytuft (iberis)	Chrysanthemum (many varieties)	Delphinium (species varieties)
Chrysanthemum (cushion varieties)	Columbine (aquilegia)	Foxglove (some varieties such as Excelsior hybrids)*
Cinquefoil (potentilla)	Coreopsis	Goldenrod (solidago)
Cranesbill geranium	Coral bells (heuchera)	Helenium
Crocus (bulb)	Delphinium	Heliopsis
Dwarf iris varieties	Gaillardia	Heliotrope (centranthus)
Feverfew	Gas plant (dictamnus)	Hollyhock (*Althea rosea*)*
Flax (linum)	Iris	Hibiscus
Grape hyacinth (bulb)	Foxglove (digitalis)*	Iris (spuria and Japanese)
Lavender	Lilies (many varieties)	Liatris (gayfeather)
Narcissi (miniature varieties; bulbs)	Loosestrive (lythrum)	Lilies (many hybrid varieties)
Painted daisy (pyrethrum)	Peony	Lupine
Pinks (dianthus)	Poppy (papaver)	Mullein (verbascum)
Phlox (*Phlox subulata*)	Phlox	Phlox
Plumbago (dwarf)	Rudbeckia	Sunflower (helianthus)
Salvia, perennial blue sage	Shasta daisy	Thermopsis (Carolina lupine)
Silver Mound (artemisia)	Spiderwort (tradescantia)	Yarrow (achillea, variety Coronation Gold)
Stokesia (Stoke's aster)	Tulips	Yucca
Tulip (botanical varieties; bulb)		*Biennial
Veronica (some varieties)		

summer peers. To get good bloom each year from chrysanthemums, you must lift each clump in the spring and divide it into several parts. Discard the old, woody center and replant the divisions.

Few perennial borders would be complete without chrysanthemums because they take over when the season is ending for most perennials. And, again, there are early, mid- and late types of chrysanthemums from which to choose. If you live where the first freeze comes early, choose early-flowering varieties for mounds of color before heavy frost.

Consult the lists shown on the facing page to help you plan a perennial border for a sunny area. By all means, include some peonies, daylilies, and chrysanthemums.

So that each may show off to best advantage, find out how high the plant grows when it's mature. The table helps you do this. However, many perennials come in a wide range of hybrids, some of which may be much taller or much shorter than the average member of the family. So use the table as a guide, but also check seed and plantsmen's data on heights before you place new plants in your border.

For additional help in planning a border of mixed perennials, consult pages 28 and 29. They include plans that guarantee the longest possible bloom. In a perennial border, something should always be in bloom!

Soft Whisper daylily has ruffled, peach blooms. Flowers are six inches across. A mid-season variety, it re-blooms in fall.

For Shady Spots

Although the list of shade-loving perennials is not as long as the one for the sun-loving varieties, there are still some great choices for your garden. Notice that some of the perennials listed for sunny beds on the preceding pages are also listed below. These plants, though they prefer sun and bloom more generously in it, will grow well but bloom less prolifically in partial shade.

A partially shaded planting area is one that receives some sun—perhaps only morning or late afternoon sun or filtered sunlight during the day. Under these conditions, the plants listed are well worth growing for the seasonal color they offer.

At the top of the list are the spring flowering bulbs, particularly the small ones, such as crocus, scilla, grape hyacinths, botanical tulips, fritillaria, snow drop, *Iris reticulata* and danfordiae, anemone blanda, and winter aconite. These will receive enough sun before trees have leafed out to build up energy for next year's bloom. Choose Virginia bluebells to accompany spring bulbs and other perennial plantings. They die back quickly and their foliage disappears early, so you might like to plant them in grassy areas under trees, as well as in a bed of perennials.

If you've never grown astilbes, make this the year to do it. Most varieties are winter hardy from Zone 4 south. They put up spikes of bloom in June and July, then bush out with attractive lacy foliage. Use astilbes in groups of three or more in the perennial border or massed in shady areas. You'll find them in white, red, salmon, rose, cream, and pink. They also like a damp location and are not fussy about soil.

A number of the plants that grow well in partial shade are also great ground covers. Often, grass won't prosper in the shady spots under trees, but some of the perennials listed here will. Among them are hosta and wild ginger. For more about these plants and others in the list, see the section entitled "ABC's" (pages 62 to 79). You'll find information on vines that can be used as ground covers. Many vines are sprawling rather than climbing in habit and require very little maintenance. Use vines to stabilize banks and eliminate a lot of mowing.

APPROXIMATE BLOOM DATES

Spring *February through early May*	Summer *Mid-May through August*	Fall *Late August to Frost*
Alkanet (anchusa)	Astilbe	Aster, hardy (Michaelmas daisy)
Anemone canadensis	Columbine (aquilegia)	Christmas rose (helleborus)
Crocus (bulb)	Coral bells (heuchera)	Daylily (hemerocallis)
Bleeding heart	Cyclamen (hardy varieties	(late-season varieties)
Dwarf iris	such as *C. Europaeum*)	Sedum
Grape hyacinth (muscari; bulb)	Daylily (hemerocallis)	Tradescantia (Blue Stone)
Hyacinth (bulb)	Globe thistle (echinops)	
Lily-of-the-valley (pips)	Hosta	**Note:** Many of the "summer"
Phlox subulata	Lobelia	perennials will continue to
Primrose (primula)	Phlox	bloom until frost if dead
Scilla siberica (bulb)	Rudbeckia	flowers are regularly
Tulip (botanical varieties; bulb)	Spiderwort (*tradescantia*)	removed and the plant is
Viola		not allowed to go to seed.
Virginia bluebells (mertensia)		A few of the early varieties,
		such as violas, may well have
		a second bloom in the fall if
		the weather is cool and the
		moisture supply sufficient.

Bright foliage and flower-laden spikes of the new hostas add colors and variegations to shaded areas of the garden.

How to Plan Perennial Borders

A successful perennial border should have that carefully planned, un-planned look, with plants arranged informally and spaced to show off their best. There's more involved than filling the bed with plants, short ones in front, tall ones behind.

Most perennials bloom for just a few weeks, so you must also consider foliage textures, blending of colors, and even distribution of color across the bed throughout the season. If all the flowers bloom at the same time, the border is drab much of the year; choosing plants for season-long color is your most important task.

The best way to keep borders bright all season long is to include annuals in your plan, as we have done here. You also get early color by planting spring-flowering bulbs in the areas where the annuals are to be planted later. The spring-flowering bulbs can be planted quite close to

SUNNY PERENNIAL BORDER

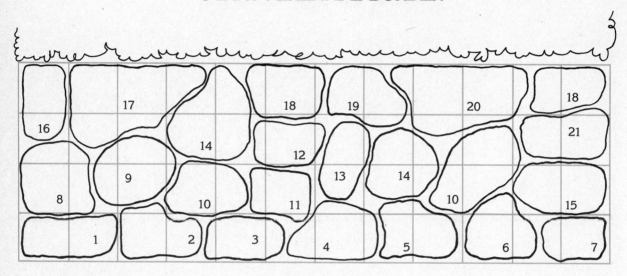

Front-of-the-Border
1. Species tulips (8)
   Dwarf zinnias later (8)
2. Alyssum, Basket-of-gold (3)
3. Crocus (12)
   Petunias later (4)
4. Artemisia, Silver Mound (3)
5. English daisy (5)
6. Creeping phlox (3)
7. Daffodils (8)
   Dwarf marigolds later (5)
8. Daffodils (10)
   Tall marigolds later (8)

Mid-Border
9. Peony (1)
10. Tulips (10)
    Tall zinnias later (8)
11. Cushion mum (1)
12. Phlox (3)
13. Yarrow (3)
14. Daylily (3)
15. Asters (2)

Back-of-the-Border
16. Solidago (3)
17. Delphinium (6)
18. Lily (3)
19. Rudbeckia (4)
20. Hollyhock (8)

Note: Our plans are shown as rectangles, but can easily be adapted to any shape you prefer. By simply expanding some planting areas or adding plants, you can widen any section to get an undulating edge. If you want a wider border, put a flagstone or patio-block walk along the back of the border, which will allow you to work the border from the back and will keep the soil from being walked on and packed down.

perennials with arching stems, such as peonies and mums. The foliage covers the ripened bulb foliage in late spring.

To emphasize the informal nature of the border, plan areas of plants, rather than single plants scattered throughout; usually three to five plants of a variety, grouped together, will make a good showing. And don't set the plants in rows. Plant them in the shape of a triangle or in no par-ticular shape at all. Of course, some plants that grow quite large, such as peonies, should be planted singly.

The depth of your flower border is important, too, if you have access for tending it from just one side. A depth of four feet, as shown on the plans, *below,* is ideal. With this depth, there's enough space for tapering the heights of plants from the front to the back of the border and to work from one side. The borders here are 12 feet long, but if you want yours longer or shorter, repeat or decrease plant groupings to fit the desired length.

Space plants so your border looks full but not crowded. Each plant or grouping should have room to display its flowers naturally, without a squeezed-in look. In both plans, the lists of plants are only suggestions. For each one, there are many more that would work equally well, or include some of your old favorites.

PARTIAL SHADE PERENNIAL BORDER

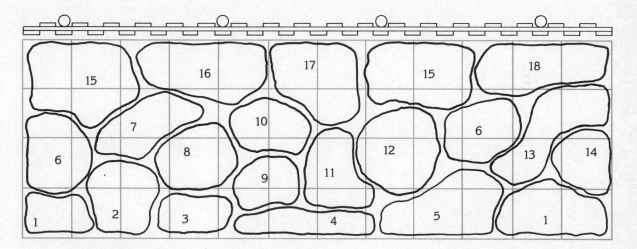

Front-of-the-Border
1. Species tulips (8)
   Wax begonias later (3)
2. Hosta, decorata (3)
3. Dwarf ferns (3)
4. Crocus, mixed (24)
   Dwarf impatiens later (5)
5. Wild ginger (3)

Mid-Border
6. Astilbe (3)
7. Daffodils (10)
   Feverfew later (5)
8. Tulips (10)
   Tall impatiens later (4)
9. Hosta, kabitan (3)
10. Bleeding heart (1)
11. Daffodils (12)
12. Hosta, *Fortunei albo-marginata* (3)
13. Tulips (12) Tall impatiens later
14. Hosta, lancifolia (1)

Back-of-the-Border
15. Fern, Lady fern (3)
16. Monarda (3)
17. Hosta, sieboldiana (1)
18. Lythrum (3)

Note: "Partial shade" as used here means the location receives morning and perhaps late afternoon sun but not midday sun. If shade is not too dense, daylilies are an excellent choice for back-of-the-border plantings; they will not bloom as heavily as in full sun but will perform adequately. Other plants that should be in every shade border are the calidium and coleus. Their bright foliage is invaluable for season-long color.

HARDY BULBS

To Brighten Your Garden

To northern gardeners, few sights are so thrilling as the first crocus poking its head through the snow, soon to be followed by scillas, grape hyacinths, narcissus, and tulips. They say loud and clear that spring is here again, and another garden season's begun.

Southern gardeners must grow tulips as annuals, because they require a long period of cold weather to bloom the following year. But by buying bulbs and storing them in the refrigerator until December, you can plant them outdoors so they'll bloom along with the azaleas. The pictures and text on these and the following six pages are aimed at persuading you that both hardy and tender bulbs deserve places of honor in your garden. The garden scene pictured on the facing pages gives you an idea of what a mixed border of narcissus, daffodils, and tulips can do to lift springtime spirits. Daffodils are also members of the narcissus family, and these easy-to-grow bulbs go on multiplying year after year. Hybrid tulips are not so obliging and tend to produce less bloom as years pass after the original planting. But their color and beauty make the effort of digging them up and replacing them from time to time a worthwhile venture. According to the old saying, a spring without bulbs is like a day without sunshine.

Plant Once for Years of Bloom

Once planted, hardy bulbs come up year after year with little fuss or bother. Feed them during the spring and mulch them during the summer, and each year they will reward you with beautiful blooms.

Lilies, the aristocrats of many a perennial border, are almost startling in their beauty. Plant them where the drainage is good, and remember they like to have "heads in the sun, feet in the shade."

Lilies are not the only hardy bulbs for summer, though the various kinds of lilies do dominate the scene. For early summer also consider the allium (its name is the Latin word for garlic), which has been hybridized to give a number of varieties with dense,

huge balls of colorful bloom atop strong stems two to four feet tall. All members of this genus need well-drained, light soil and a sunny spot.

For late summer bloom from hardy bulbs, rely on the Resurrection Lily (Lycoris) and Colchicum.

Resurrection lilies should be planted in the fall. The following spring, strap-like foliage will appear, ripen, and then disappear. On a day in August, the bloom spikes will thrust up, and lavender or crimson flowers will open on tall stems.

Colchicum bulbs need partial shade. Plant in August for bloom in September. Vase-shaped pink or violet flowers will open at ground level soon after you plant the bulbs.

Visualize up to ten of these magnificent lilies crowning each six-foot stem. It is one of the Imperial Crimson strain.

A GUIDE TO BULB CULTURE

Flowering Period	Genus and Species or Variety	Average Height at Maturity (Inches)	Depth of Planting (Inches)	Space Between Bulbs (Inches)
Very Early Spring *March 15-30*	Crocus chrysanthus	3-4	4	2-3
	Crocus tomasinianus	3-4	4	3-4
	Eranthis species	3-4	4	2-3
	Galanthus species	3-4	4	2-3
	Iris reticulata	4-5	4	2-3
	Scilla tubergeniana	4-6	4	3-4
Early Spring *March 31- April 20*	Anemone blanda	3-4	4	2
	Chionodoxa species	5-8	4	2-3
	Crocus flavus	3-4	4	3-4
	Crocus vernus	4-6	4	3-4
	Muscari azureum	4-5	4	1-2
	Narcissus cyclamineus	10-14	6	4-6
	Puschkinia scilloides	4-6	4	3-4
	Scilla siberica	4-6	4	3-4
Mid-Spring *April 21-May 15*	*Erythronium "Pagoda"	8-12	3	3-4
	Fritillaria imperialis	25-30	6	8
	Hyacinth Blue Jacket	10-12	6	9
	Narcissus jonquilla	10-14	6	3-4
	Narcissus triandrus Thalia	10-14	6	4-6
	Narcissus	8-10	6	4-5
Late Spring *May 16-June 5*	Allium aflatunense	26-30	4	4
	Allium karataviense	8-10	4	6-8
	*Camassia quamash	12-16	6	4
	*Ixiolirion tataricum	15-17	4	6
	Narcissus Baby Moon	10-14	6	4-5
	Ornithogalum umbellatum	8-10	4	3-4
Early Summer *June-July*	Allium giganteum	40-48	6	6
	Lilium candidum	36-50	**	10-12
	Lilium enchantment	36-40	8-10	10-12
	Lilium regale	48-72	4-8	10-12
	Mid-century hybrid lilies			
	L. Chinook	40-48	4-8	6-7
	L. Cinnabar	30-36	4-8	6-7
	L. Imperial Crimson strain	60-72	4-8	6-7
Late Summer *August- September*	Colchicum	no stem	6-8	8-10
	Lilium auratum platyphyllum	60-72	4-8	6-7
	L. Jamboree Strain	60-72	4-8	6-7
	L. speciosum rubrum	36-48	6-8	6-7
	Lycoris squamigera	24-36	6-8	6-8

*Not reliably winter-hardy north of Zone 5

TENDER BULBS

To Brighten Your Summer

In gardeners' terms, the tender bulbs are those which, in climates where temperatures sink to freezing and below, must be planted in spring, after the ground has warmed. They will produce generous bloom during summer months but must be lifted in the fall and stored in a cool, dry place for the winter. Come spring they can be replanted in your garden and will give you another year of pleasure.

We've been using the term "bulbs" a bit loosely thus far. Some you'll want to grow are really bulbs (peruvian daffodils), some are technically corms (gladiolus), some are tubers (cannas), and some are rhizomes or tuberous roots (tuberous begonias). But they look like bulbs and, in cold climates, cannot be left outdoors in winter.

Dwarf dahlias (pictured on the facing page) grow from tubers. They're great for planters, borders, and low hedges. And they bloom generously from midsummer until the first frost. You can cut them as you please; new buds keep coming. These bushy little plants measure one to two feet high. Grow them from seed or buy tuberous roots. Set the roots five inches apart in a sunny location. If you start from seed, thin seedlings to from ten to 12 inches apart. In cold areas, dig dahlias in the fall. Wash off soil with a firm stream of water and pack as soon as dry in dry vermiculite, sand, or plastic bags in a cool but frost-free spot. Don't separate clumps until the spring planting; then cut them apart, making sure each tuber has part of last year's stem and at least one bud or "eye."

Tender Bulbs for Shady Spots

Caladiums are obliging foliage plants that are perfect for color in shade. Leaves can be all green and white, or green with pink or red markings.

If your garden is shaded by big trees, don't think you can't use colorful plants. Some of the greatest garden beauties, such as the caladiums and tuberous begonias pictured here, can only be grown in light shade.

Combine these exciting plants with shade-loving annuals and perennials, and you can rival the color in the sunniest gardens. And, remember, a shaded garden is more comfortable to work in or sit in on summer days.

Buy young plants of tuberous begonias or caladiums, or start tubers indoors in late February or March to have blooming-size plants when warm weather arrives.

Tuberous begonias grow best in cool areas with moist air, so a light misting every day will be helpful. Caladiums can take heat better than tuberous begonias, but they will require more frequent watering.

Tubers of these begonias probably will show tiny pink buds on their upper rims. To plant, set tubers in flats filled with vermiculite or a 50-50 mixture of vermiculite and peat moss. In any case, provide for drainage, because at this stage tubers rot easily. Space them three inches apart, and cover their tops with ½ inch of the rooting mixture. Roots will grow from both the top and base of the tuber. Place flats in bright light, but not in direct sun.

When two or three leaves have formed, transplant into pots. After nighttime temperatures have remained at, or above, 50 degrees (Fahrenheit) for about a week, you can plant outside. Either remove it from the pot and plant in garden beds, or put it into planters. If you want to bring the plant inside for the winter, transplant the begonia or caladium into an eight-inch pot, and

Exciting blends of colors make the picotee begonias garden standouts.

sink the pot in the soil. This makes it easy to lift the plant in late summer with minimal damage to the roots.

In choosing outdoor locations for tuberous begonias and caladiums, pick those that receive dappled sunlight, never deep shade.

Add quantities of organic matter to the soil for your tender bulbs. Dig in well-rotted cow manure, leaf mold, garden loam, and peat moss. Add some sand to assure good drainage.

Put in stakes for the heavy top growth of tuberous begonias at planting time. Putting stakes in later can damage many roots. Tie stems to stakes with soft plastic tape, not wired strips, because the tender stems can be cut by a narrow tie.

Tuberous begonias are ravenous eaters, so established plants should get a weekly feeding of balanced plant food. As flower buds begin to show color, shift to fish emulsion, using a teaspoon to a gallon of water. Give each plant about a pint of this mixture each week.

Caladiums and tuberous begonias have few insect and disease pests once they have been planted outside, but a little preventive spraying or dusting every other week will keep the foliage and blossoms in prime condition. Direct the spray or dust onto the soil and base of the stems, rather than douse the entire plant with the material.

Bring your potted begonias and caladiums indoors in late summer or very early fall before early dormancy starts—it takes the plants several weeks to readjust once dormancy begins. Lift the plants from garden beds or planters when the first warnings of light frost are given. Take into basement or garage and allow to dry. When the stem drops off, remove the tuber from the soil and wash clean.

Remove all the roots and store the tubers in boxes or coffee cans filled with dry sand. Leave the lids off.

In March of the following year, remove the tubers from storage and follow the procedures for new tubers. Your tubers will increase in size and vigor each year.

The flowers of tuberous begonias, magnificent in color and form, are tempting to pick. Their stems are short, so their uses are limited. Float in a shallow bowl or large snifter. Resist the temptation to cut a length of stem for arranging. You'll sacrifice many future blossoms if you do.

Caladium leaves work beautifully into many types of flower arrangements, but pick them sparingly, if at all. The caladium flowers are unusual but not especially attractive. Pick them off and discard as soon as they appear, so the strength of the plant goes into the foliage.

Tuberous begonias offer a wide range of colors and flower forms, including: camellia, carnation, rose, and gardenia.

TREES

For Trouble-free Landscapes

"Plant in haste and repent at leisure" is an apt adage if you're talking about trees. The sapling you plant today is going to become a major part of your landscape in ten years or less. So take your time before deciding what to plant, and by all means, think carefully of its size at maturity. If you're planting primarily for shade, make sure that where the tree is placed will give you shade where you want it in the summer. Plant trees where they will supply natural air conditioning for house and patio in hot weather. Think, too, of the beauty to be gained by planting small ornamental and flowering trees, such as crab apples (choose non-fruiting kinds, unless you want to make jelly), saucer magnolia, redbud, fringe tree, and silk-tree. Or choose fruit-bearing trees, such as the lovely old specimen opposite; ornamental pear trees and cherry trees also bring a glorious spring bloom into the picture. For added help on choosing trees, see pages 38 and 39; for their care and pruning, see pages 84 and 85.

Before you make any final choices, try to visit parks in your part of the country and drive around residential areas, observing what your favorite trees look like when they're mature.

Trees for a Trouble-Free Landscape

Your first consideration when planning a garden should be trees. This is important for older homes where there are possibly some existing trees, but it is imperative for a new house built on a treeless site.

The reason for haste in planting trees is simple. Of all the plants in your yard they take the longest time to reach functional sizes, so the sooner you plant them, the sooner you'll enjoy their beauty and shade. If you don't have the money to buy a 20-foot tree for immediate effect, buy the biggest one you can afford, even if it is just a whip four or five feet tall. With proper care, it may catch up with the bigger trees in a few years. the point is: get the trees *started*. If you wait until you can afford the larger sizes, your yard may be treeless for many years.

If you haven't shopped for trees in recent years, you'll be amazed at the choices. It may take a little searching, but you can find a tree to fit just about any plan you have in mind. There are many shapes in all categories of deciduous trees: spreading vase shapes, pyramidal, columnar, oval, and weeping forms.

Aside from their aesthetic value and the comforting shade a tree offers for the patio or garden, the expense of heating and cooling a house has become an important factor in the placement and choice of trees.

Large deciduous shade trees planted to the south and west of a house can greatly reduce the price of cooling your home in the summer. And in winter, when the leaves are gone, the warming sun can reach walls, windows, and the roof, thereby cutting heating bills considerably. Low-branched evergreen trees planted to the north and west can cut winter winds that are capable of penetrating every crevice in the house.

Evergreen trees offer a wide choice of sizes, colors, and textures, too, although most are pyramidal or columnar in shape. Included here are the pines, spruces, hemlocks, junipers, and firs. Use them primarily for background, screening, or windbreaks, but don't neglect them as specimen plants in an open area of lawn, if you have enough space. (Circle a garden hose to fit a 20-foot diameter to get an idea of the eventual spread of the tree's ground-sweeping branches. If it will crowd flower borders or sidewalks, abandon the idea of planting an evergreen specimen. Try an ornamental flowering tree instead.) The Colorado blue spruce is the best evergreen to use as a specimen; the grafted varieties, Moerheim and Koster, are well worth the extra expense for their intense, gray-blue color.

Don't just plant *a* tree. Study nursery catalogs, and visit your local nurseries to learn about the many trees available and to see many of them firsthand. Nurserymen are more than happy to help you choose the appropriate tree for a particular situation. If your garden is large and you are not knowledgeable about gardening, hire a landscape architect to help select trees or plan your entire garden. A landscape architect can save money for you in the long run and eliminate many expensive mistakes—particularly when choosing trees. If you make a bad choice, you have to live with the mistake for many years. The same holds true when you select shrubs for a privacy border or plants for foundation planting. A landscape architect is a professional who can make your entire garden something special and not just a hodgepodge of plants.

For years, the old, short-lived Lombardy poplar was the only columnar tree commonly available, and as a screen it was used extensively across the backs of many gardens. Today, there are many beautiful, long-lived columnar trees. Choose a columnar oak, crab apple, maple, cherry, or even a ginkgo to serve as a background screen or as an accent plant in your shrub border. The crab apples and cherries are especially beautiful when they bloom in the spring.

If you are unfortunate enough to have utility wires draped along your side of the street, select trees that grow just 25 to 30 feet high. At maturity, these trees need no trimming that would distort their natural shapes. They also serve handsomely in other areas of the garden where a big tree is not desired. If you plant large shade trees throughout your yard, be prepared, eventually, to change the entire character of your garden. You will gradually go from sun-loving perennials and annuals to plants that prefer shade. The reverse of this happened when the Dutch elm disease spread across America. Former shade gardens were exposed to the blazing sun, and plants tender to the sun died from the exposure and had to be replaced with varieties more tolerant of sunlight.

Ornamental trees are a special breed. The average city lot offers space for several of these. There are varieties that bloom in spring, summer, and fall—and in a variety of colors and shapes. The crab apples, cherries, and redbud are spring favorites; the golden chain tree waits until summer to suspend its chains of yellow blossoms. In fall, the shade and ornamental trees alike produce a spectacle of yellow, orange, and red leaf color.

Flowering trees can be important parts of your shrub borders because they add height in certain areas for an undulating effect. As specimens in an open lawn or in planting areas of a patio, they can't be surpassed. Don't neglect to work one of these ornamental beauties into the foundation planting at the front of your house. So long as you plant them at least eight feet from the house, there is little danger of damage to the foundation. When planted near the house, a flowering tree helps you gain privacy, breaks the long lines of the house, shades the front walk, and is just plain pretty.

Of course, planting too many trees can cause problems, too. Grass won't grow under a heavy leaf cover, and light can't reach windows, so rooms are dark and gloomy. Space major shade trees at least 50 feet apart.

If you think you aren't going to stay in a house long enough to benefit from a shade tree, plant one anyway. Trees add greatly to the value of the property, and the house may sell more quickly because of them.

The crepe myrtle is an outstanding tree for the southern garden. Its bright clusters of flowers appear in summer.

SHRUBS

That Give You Yards of Flowers

If you want large numbers of flowers for garden color or bouquets, you won't find a more generous source than flowering shrubs. Many cover themselves with bloom for several weeks. And when you consider that quite a few are eight feet tall and wide, or even bigger, that's a lot of flowers. A mature lilac or rhododendron in full bloom is a sight not easily forgotten. The smaller shrubs, though offering a lesser quantity of bloom, are invaluable in every part of the garden.

There are three basic types of shrubs to add spice and variety to your landscape. The evergreens, including junipers and yews, offer year-round greenery to your garden scheme, especially in foundation plantings. Broad-leaved evergreens, such as mahonia and holly, keep their leafy foliage all year long, for textured contrast in leaf and shape with the needle evergreens. The deciduous shrubs lose their leaves in the fall, but through most of the year their flowers and foliage give them important status in the landscape.

To gain seclusion for outdoor living areas, a shrub border is your least expensive choice. By carefully choosing shrubs for a privacy screen around your property, you can have a beautiful transition of flowers and foliage textures all season long.

Privacy You Can Grow

Dense growth makes privets (ligustrum) a good choice for clipped hedges. Amur privet is extremely hardy. Plant California privet in areas with warm winters.

A number of shrub roses make choice hedges. If they're planted along sidewalks, set them back about three feet from the walk so the thorns won't bother passersby. In cold zones, Eutin, Betty Prior are hardy.

This hardy rugosa, F. J. Grootendorst, blooms heavily in June, intermittently afterward. Set plants three feet apart.

If you want large returns with little effort, consider a hedge that needs little pruning.

If you prefer a natural or informal landscape or the style of your house suggests it, several of the plants listed, *opposite,* as well as many listed in the column at right can provide a good measure of privacy without your doing a lot of pruning. The common Japanese barberry, which grows to five or six feet, is worth considering. Only if set close to a walk or path will you have to do much pruning—its thorns can tear skin and clothing in these locations. Mock-orange, in its taller form, is another tall hedge that needs little trimming. And it has the advantage of offering fragrant spring bloom. Sweet mock-orange — *Philadelphus coronarius*—grows from six to eight feet tall and bears large white, fragrant blooms in May or June. Among other flowering shrubs you'll like as privacy hedges are Rose-of-Sharon, beauty bush, and forsythia. These grow tall and wide but need no pruning if you have space for them.

Do not shear all shrubs as you do a formal hedge. To retain the informal look most shrubs require, cut out individual branches to maintain the

Name	Mature height unclipped	Minimum height clipped	Spacing
Dwarf highbush cranberry	2'-3'	1½'	1'
Dwarf mock-orange	3'	1½'	1'
Lodense privet	3'	1½'	1'
Dwarf ninebark	4'	2'	1½'
Froebel spirea	4'	2½'	1½'
Korean boxwood*	4'-5'	1½'	1½'
Alpine currant	4'	3'	1½'
Japanese barberry	5'-6'	3'	1½'
Dwarf winged euonymus	6'	3'	2'
Dwarf Japanese quince	6'	3'	2'
Japanese yew*	10'	4'	3'
Amur privet	15'	3½'	2'
Amur maple	20'	4½'	3'
*Evergreen			

shrub's size and natural character.

For lower hedges in areas with mild winters, weigela, carlesi viburnum, and slender deutzia are all rewarding. They flower freely in spring, especially if unpruned.

Recommended flowering shrubs for low hedges in colder zones are Anthony Waterer spirea and February daphne. Daphne's fragrant bloom appears in early spring. This spirea gives you a month or more of summer bloom. Neither needs much attention once established.

Flowering quince is another popular hedge. Its bright spring flowers and glossy leaves are held close to the stems—excellent for spring bouquets. The foliage remains shiny all summer, in spite of heat and dry weather.

Oregon-grape mahonia makes a handsome hedge, but it is not suited to growing in full sun. Too much sun burns its leaves. It grows to a height of five or six feet and is hardy from Zone five southward. A broadleaved-evergreen, it is especially desirable in winter.

There are many shrubs you can use to divide your property from a neighbor's or to provide privacy. The best way to choose the right shrub is to find one the ultimate height of which is close to the height you have in mind.

For example, if you want a low hedge, don't choose a highbush cranberry; it reaches 12 feet at maturity. However, if you want the privacy a tall hedge can give you, this viburnum could be an excellent choice.

When you purchase plants to use as hedges, bare-root specimens may be the best buy. Be sure roots are well developed and are moist and supple. Plant bare-root shrubs as early in spring as possible. If you order young plants from a catalog, make certain the variety you choose is hardy in your temperature zone.

When ready to plant, dig a trench as long as you want it and deep enough so plants can be set at the depth they grew in the nursery. As you dig the trench, soak the roots of the plants in water. To survive, plants must be watered regularly during the first growing season.

Consult the chart, *right*, for more suggestions on shrubs you can grow as hedges.

Name	Height (in feet)	*Hardiness	Comments
TALL Crapemyrtle	20	15°/20°	Pink, white, red, or lavender flowers. Summer bloom.
Rose-of-sharon	12	−5°/−10°	Large blue, pink, white, or purple flowers in summer.
Chinese lilac	15	−10°/−20°	One of the best flowering hedges. Purple flowers.
Common privet	15	−20°	Excellent hedge for formal trimming.
Beauty bush	10	−10°	Small pink flowers. Graceful, arching shrub.
Border forsythia	9	−10°	Yellow, bell-shaped flowers in spring. Upright growth.
Highbush cranberry	12	−15°/−20°	Leaves maple-like, large white flower clusters. Bright red fruit.
Pink double-flowering plum	10	−10°	Pink flowers appear before leaves. Textured foliage.
MEDIUM Vanicek weigela	5	0°	Dark red flowers in spring. Good specimen shrub.
Viburnum carlesii	5	−5°	Clusters of white fragrant blooms in spring. Foliage turns red in fall.
Slender deutzia	3-6	−10°/−15°	Small, graceful shrub with white blooms in late spring.
Korean barberry	6	−10°	Useful as thorny hedge. Red foliage in fall.
Mock-orange	6-8	−10°	White, fragrant blooms in early summer. Hedge or as specimen plant.
Bush cinquefoil	4	−35°	Single yellow flowers, early spring. Useful foundation or border shrub.
Dwarf flowering almond	4	−10°	Large, double-pink flowers early spring. Use in shrub border or as specimen.
Glossy abelia	5	0°	Pink flowers during summer. Fall color, bronze to purple. Makes dense hedge.
LOW Froebel spirea	4	−10°	Flat, purplish-red flowers during summer. Useful as foundation or border plant.
Hills of Snow hydrangea	3	0°/−5°	Large balls of white blooms early summer.
Anthony Waterer spirea	2	0°/−5°	Rosy crimson flowers in mid-June and early July.
February daphne	4-5	−10°/−15°	Fragrant purple flowers in early February, March.
Cream broom	4-6	10°/15°	Dense, compact shrub. Creamy-yellow flowers. Best in full sun, sandy soils.
Dwarf flowering quince	3	−5°/10°	Thrives in almost any soil, heat, or drought.

*Hardiness: Minimum temperatures

VINES

The Great Cover-Ups

Use vines to solve tough garden problems. If you have a stark fence or wall or if you need shade or privacy for a patio, think of vines. Both perennial and annual vines come in a variety of leaf sizes, bloom colors, and light requirements. Look about a little, and you're sure to find the right vine for the job.

The clematis, among perennial vines, has few rivals for size and beauty of bloom, and it's hardy from Zone three south. But it does need sunlight. For either sun or light shade, consider the trumpet vine, *Campsis radicans, opposite.* Tough and dependable, it blooms throughout the summer. Clusters of bright orange, trumpet-shaped flowers peek through the thick mat of foliage, which is excellent for shade or screening. Grow against masonry walls or trellis only; the heavy growth can damage wood siding.

Among the annuals, great favorites are the morning glory and giant moonflower. Both need a sunny location, but one blooms by day, the other by night. Both are vigorous vines that grow quickly, so have supports in place at planting time. Morning glory vines, like the one pictured, *opposite,* grow from eight to ten feet tall. To get the longest possible season of bloom from them, start seed indoors four to six weeks before the last expected frost. Set young plants into pots or the spot outdoors where they will grow when the ground is warm.

Quick Vines from Seed

The Black-eyed Susan vine, Thunbergia alata, *is an annual vine that grows in sun or partial shade. Many orange, daisy-like blooms appear during the summer. Start seed indoors in March.*

For fast growth and season-long bloom, annuals can't be beat. This holds true for annual vines, too. Perennial vines generally take several years to make much of a showing, but the annuals make their full growth and bloom fully in one season, so they have to hurry.

All the popular annual vines bloom beautifully from early summer right up to frost, so the color they add to your garden can be important to your garden color scheme. Only a few are good to pick for arrangements, but the sweet pea and climbing nasturtium are notable exceptions. The colors and fragrance of sweet pea make it a must for every garden.

To decorate a bare wall or hide an ugly view, the annual vines are hard to beat. They can climb a wire fence in short order or cover a trellis in a single season. Of course, some, like the moonflower, have big leaves and grow faster than some of the smaller types, so if it is screening you are after they are the best choice. The ultimate size of the vine is one of the considerations you will have to make when choosing a vine for a specific situation. Often, a smaller kind will be perfect for a situation that would be unsuitable for a big one.

All the annual vines must have something to climb on because they don't have holdfasts as many of the perennial vines do. A wire fence or wire trellis are perfect for the twisting stems of these climbers to hold on to as they reach upward. Heavy cord can be stretched for a single season's use. The main thing is to have the support in place when you plant the seed. Otherwise, the early growth will be a tangled mess on the ground, and the plants will never make the vertical growth they should if the support is put in too late.

Another feature of annual vines is that they are inexpensive. A packet of seed can plant an extensive area; by planting a seed every four or five inches in a row, you can have an extensive solid cover from the ground up in no time at all. To get this kind of coverage, perennials must be trained horizontally for some time. If your ultimate objective is to have a perennial vine cover an area, you can plant it where you want it and plant annual vines nearby to give temporary cover while the slower grower is getting established.

You do have to give some of the seedling vines a little help to get them started up their supports, but once begun, they wind their way up on their own. Often, just winding the first growth into place is all that's needed.

Most packets contain more seed than you'll ever need. This allows you ample to gamble on an early planting. If these fail, because of a late freeze or because the soil is too cold for germination, there are more for a later planting when the weather is ideal. Any extras can be planted in another area needing cover, or try a few planted without support to use as a ground cover.

Vines don't like to be moved after growth is established, so plant them where they are to finish their growth. Morning glories are especially hard to transplant. Some, like the morning glory, have hard-shelled seeds. To hasten germination of these, soak the seeds overnight in warm water, or shake them in a glass jar that has been lined with a piece of sandpaper. The scraping will wear down the tough cover. Annual vines are invaluable in small gardens. They give maximum color in a narrow, vertical area so there is room for more plants. Adjacent walls and fences can be made to come alive with their colorful flowers. Grown on an overhead arbor, they both screen the view from nearby neighbors and provide cooling shade for deck or patio.

If you want the vines and don't have a wall or garden structure to cover, set a tall post in a sunny spot and plant an annual vine at its base. The vines will soon make a column of lush green foliage and a wealth of colorful flowers. Or a small dead tree can be given new "life" for a season or two by covering it with annual vines; this stand-in for the real thing will get you by until the tree replacing it gets started nearby.

As with all other plants, annual vines prefer a well-prepared bed of good soil. Nasturtiums and morning glories aren't as choosy as most of the others, but they, too, respond to good soil. All the annual vines prefer sunny locations. Usually, a half day of sun is sufficient, but the more sun, the better. Get more details on vines and soil care on pages 88 through 91. And check the listing and descriptions of the easiest-to-grow annual vines in the "ABCs" section.

A delicious substitute for the usual annual vine are the vegetables and fruits you can train on a fence or trellis. Climbing pole and lima beans, cucumbers, small-fruited watermelons, and cantalopes climb high for good screening and provide the benefits of fresh fruits and vegetables. Or try the long, rambling squash varieties as vine substitutes. The heavy fruits of some of the above will need some support. Use squares of cloth or old stockings as hammocks to hold them up while they ripen. All but the beans will need help in climbing; just keep threading new growth through openings in the wire. The beans will need no help in finding their way up.

Although they aren't vines, tomatoes can serve as one. Plant tall-growing kinds, such as Big Boy and Early Girl, close to a wall or fence, and train growth tightly against it. Keep suckers picked off, so the plant doesn't bush out. When limited to two or three main stems, a tomato can easily climb to six feet in height and have a spread of three feet.

Morning glories give you more color per square foot than any other vine. And they bloom in red, pink, white, or blue all summer.

GROUND COVERS

The Backbone of a Low-care Garden

Slopes too steep to mow and hard-to-get-at corners can take more than their fair share of your time. Any easy way to eliminate these energy-wasters is to use ground covers. If the areas are in the shade, there are attractive plants ready to do the job. Try *Vinca minor,* a carpet of common violets, or wild ginger. If the spots are mostly sunny, choose Hall's honeysuckle, Japanese fleece flower, or Baltic or English ivy. All of these will spread to cover the area with a thick blanket of foliage that will smother weeds and beautifully cover the problem area.

The hardy ground cover pictured, *opposite,* is Japanese fleece flower, *Polygonum cuspidatum 'compactum.'* It's unbeatable on steep and sunny banks because it takes full sun and dry weather in stride, although its uses are somewhat limited because its mature height is two feet. It spreads rapidly, so plant only where there's plenty of room or in a confined space that will keep it within bounds.

For more help in choosing the right ground cover, see the pages immediately following these and the information on specific ground covers included in the "ABCs" section on page 78.

Ground Covers

In sun, ajuga bears spires of purplish-blue bloom during the spring; in shade, less bloom. Its glossy leaves and low-growing habit make it attractive.

Count on ground covers to add beauty to bare spots beneath shrubs and trees. Those pictured here are well known and widely used, but less conventional ground covers include mass plantings of such annuals as dwarf marigolds or portulaca (in sun); hosta; and perennial ferns (in shade). Do not use annuals as a ground cover on slopes. The soil will be subject to erosion during winter months when the plants are dead.

Once planted and established, perennial ground covers require little attention from you. The thick foliage smothers most of the weeds, and they are, in general, drought resistant and hardy.

Perennials protect slopes from erosion year round. As with most pe-

rennial plants you expect to grow in the same area for a number of years, careful preparation of soil is important. Be generous with compost and peat moss, spading them deeply into the garden soil. Spacing of new plants depends on how big they'll get. As a rule, low-growing kinds (ajuga, for example) are best spaced eight to 12 inches from each other. Taller kinds, such as Hall's honeysuckle and polygonum, may be spaced from two to three feet apart.

Many ground covers, though they may seem expensive when you buy them, will spread rapidly. And you can increase your supply. Take cuttings and root them in moist vermiculite (vinca minor lends itself well to this method). Others (ajuga is

Epimedium rubrum *(ten inches) has showy foliage; it needs protection from sun.*

one; succulent hen-and-chickens, another) have offsets from the mother plant that can be cut off with a sharp knife. Make sure you get some roots along with leaves of the offset. Then set them into the ground as you did when setting out the original plantings.

To keep ground covers vigorous, give them fertilizer in early spring.

The only other regular care they will need is a thorough soaking during a prolonged spell of hot, dry weather. It's also a good idea to water them heavily during a dry fall to ensure a winter supply of moisture.

Some of the dwarf evergreens—prostrate juniper, for instance—make handsome ground covers. Space the young plants two feet apart throughout the deeply dug area. Cover the exposed ground between plants with a mulch of fir or redwood bark chunks. Bark lasts for a number of years, so the initial expense is a bit deceiving. After a year or two, simply add a small amount each year to keep the mulch at a level of two inches. Within a few years, the evergreens will form a solid cover.

By blocking sun and drying winds, this kind of mulch can reduce water losses by as much as 50 percent. It helps soil moisture and nutrients go to the roots and stems of the plants, rather than to weeds or to the air through evaporation.

Among other less commonly used ground covers are certain wildflowers. Wild ginger looks great all summer in a shady area; bloodroot foliage is an unusual and attractive plant in shade. After delicate white flowers fade, the foliage continues to grow throughout the summer, keeping its green color until the first frost.

Herbs, too, can sometimes act as ground covers. Thyme is one of the most desirable because it does well in the winter from Zone five southward. In its several varieties, thyme grows from two to 12 inches high. Planted between stepping-stones of a sunny path, a few strands will spread onto the stones. When you step on them, you release their aromatic scent. If you want to grow thyme this way, look in seed catalogs for a prostrate variety, such as *Thymus serpyllum*.

Hall's honeysuckle quickly spreads across any sunny area to form a ground cover up to two feet deep. It withstands drought well.

53

WILDFLOWERS

You Can Tame for Your Garden

Wildflowers are scattered casually throughout Nature's beautiful garden of forest and field for all to see. Many kinds—a few or a whole yardful—can be tamed and grown in your garden. The wildflowers you think of first are the delicate woodland flowers appearing in spring. But they're not limited to moist, shady spots or to spring bloom only. There are wildflowers that grow well in rocky spots, sunny open areas, or sandy locations. And countless species bloom generously in summer or fall.

All this does *not* mean you should dig them from the countryside. This is against the law in many states. Plantsmen throughout the country specialize in wildflower plants and seed; turn to them for advice. Their catalogs are filled with dependable information, including the actual name of each plant so you don't have to guess at it. Many wildflowers spread rapidly by seed or runners; your original planting will spread naturally if it is left undisturbed.

Pictured opposite is one of the springtime charmers, Adders-tongues. They are often called dog-tooth violets, although they're not related to true violets. Actually, they belong to the lily family but have violet-like blossoms held above their delicately mottled leaves.

Wildflowers

ALUMROOT (*heuchera*)
Tiny flowers on stems 16 to 36 inches tall from May to August. Needs shade and well-drained, dry soil. Multiply by seeds or root division. Mottled leaves when plant is young.

ANEMONE, RUE (*anemonella*)
Early bloom on stems 5 to 9 inches in height; white and pink in color. Bloom from March to June. Needs shade and well-drained, dry soil. Multiply by seeds or root division in the fall.

ARBUTUS, TRAILING (*epigaea*)
Tubular bloom on 3-inch plants are white and pink, blooming March to May. White berries later. Needs partial shade and well-drained, dry soil. Multiply by seeds, stem cuttings, stem layering.

BANEBERRY (*actaea*)
Small white flowers on 24-inch plants in April and May followed by red or white berries. Needs shade and moist, well-drained soil. Increase by seed and division.

BELLWORT (*uvularia*)
Yellow bloom on graceful 4- to 12-inch plants from April to June. Needs shade and well-drained, moist soil. Increase by seed and root division in fall.

BISHOP'S-CAP (*mitella*)
Tiny white bloom on 6- to 12-inch plants from April to June. Needs shade and well-drained, moist soil. Increase by seeds or root division. Keep mulched.

BLACK-EYED SUSAN (*rudbeckia*)
Daisy-like bloom on 2-foot stems in July and August. Needs sun, well-drained soil. Biennial; often self-sows.

BLOODROOT (*sanguinaria*)
Large-leaved plants 8 to 10 inches tall. Single white flowers in April and May. Needs shade and well-drained, dry soil. Increase by seeds and division.

BLUEBELLS (*mertensia*)
Tall 2-foot stems of blue flowers on 12- to 15-inch stems in April and May. Needs sun or partial shade and well-drained, moist soil. Increase by seeds or root division. Foliage dies when bloom ends.

BUTTERFLY WEED (*asclepias*)
Clusters of orange bloom on 2-foot plants in July and August. Needs sun and well-drained, dry soil. Increase by seed; old plants are hard to move.

CINQUEFOIL (*potentilla*)
Tiny white flowers on 3- to 6-inch plants in June to August. Needs shade and well-drained, dry soil. Foliage turns red in autumn. Increase by seed, stem cuttings, or division.

COLUMBINE, WILD (*aquilegia*)
Finely cut foliage and pendulous yellow and red bloom on 1- to 2-foot plants from April through July. Needs shade and well-drained, dry soil on the acid side. Increase by seeds.

CONEFLOWER, PRAIRIE (*ratibida*)
Big yellow flowers on plants to 6 feet tall from June to August. Needs sun and well-drained, dry soil. Increase by seed or root division. Showy.

CONEFLOWER, PURPLE (*echinacea*)
Large, single purple flowers on 3- to 4-foot plants from June to October. It needs sun and well-drained, dry soil. Increase by seeds or root division.

CROWFOOT, BUTTERCUP (*ranunculus*)
Small yellow flowers on 6-to 24-inch plants from April to August. It needs partial shade. Tolerant of most soil types. Propagate by seeds or division.

DOG-TOOTH VIOLET (*erythronium*)
Solitary white flowers on plants 6 inches tall in April and May. Needs shade and well-drained, moist soil. Increase from seed or offsets.

DUTCHMAN'S BREECHES (*dicentra*)
Unusually shaped white bloom in clusters on plants 6 to 12 inches tall in spring. Needs shade and well-drained, moist soil. Leaves mottled brown. Increase from seed or offsets.

EVENING PRIMROSE (*oenothera*)
Pale yellow, fragrant bloom on plants 2 to 4 feet tall in July to August. Needs sun and well-drained, dry soil. Flowers open only after sundown. Treat as a biennial. Increase from seeds.

FLAG, BLUE (*iris*)
Large blue-purple bloom on plants 2 to 3 feet tall in May and June. Needs sun and moist to wet, slightly acid soil. Propagate by division or seed.

FORGET-ME-NOT (*myosotis*)
Pale blue bloom with yellow centers on 6-inch plants. Blooms all summer. Needs sun and well-drained, moist to wet soil. Increase by division or seed.

GENTIAN, CLOSED BLUE (*gentiana*)
Tubular, violet bloom on plants 1 foot tall in August to September. Needs sun, partial shade, and well-drained, moist soil on acid side. Increase by root division or seeds.

GERANIUM, WILD (*geranium*)
Big, red-violet flowers in clusters on plants 24 inches tall. Needs shade and well-drained, moist soil. Increase by root division or seeds. Effective in mass plantings.

GINGER, WILD (*asarum*)
Inconspicuous, tubular, violet-brown flowers hidden by foliage on plants 4 to 8 inches tall, April to May. Needs shade and well-drained, moist soil. Multiply by division. Good ground cover.

HEPATICAS (*hepatica*)
Showy, rose, white, or blue bloom on short 6-inch plants from April to May. Needs shade and well-drained soil on acid side. Increase by seed or division.

JACK-IN-THE-PULPIT (*arisaema*)
Unusual vase-shaped, greenish-brown flowers on plants 3 feet tall from April to June. Red berries follow. Needs shade and well-drained, moist soil. Increase by seeds. Often self-sows.

JACOB'S-LADDER (*polemonium*)
Small clusters of blue flowers on 3-foot plants in June and July. Needs shade and well-drained, moist soil. Increase by seeds or root division.

LADY'S-SLIPPER, YELLOW (*cypripedium*)
A wild orchid, this very showy plant has yellow May bloom, often veined in blue, on plants up to 30 inches tall. Needs shade and well-drained, moist soil. Increase by root division. Top annually with a dressing of compost.

LOBELIA, BLUE (*lobelia*)
Tiny blue flowers on 2- to 3-foot plants from August to October. Plant in sun or partial shade and in moist, well-drained soil. Increase by root division, stem cuttings, or seed.

MALLOW ROSE (*hibiscus*)
Large red, pink, or white flowers on plants 6 feet tall in April and May. Needs partial to full shade and well-drained soil. Increase by division or seed.

MARIGOLD, MARSH (*caltha*)
Bright yellow clustered bloom on 2-foot plants in April to May. Needs sun and moist to wet soil. Increase by root division.

MAYAPPLE, MANDRAKE (*podophyllum*)
Single, white daisy-like bloom on 12- to 18-inch plants, April to May. Unusual umbrella-like leaves. Yellow fruit in August. Needs partial to full shade and well-drained, moist soil. Increase by seed or root division.

MEADOW-RUE, EARLY (*thalictrum*)
Small greenish-white bloom on 2-foot plants in April to May. Needs sun and well-drained, moist soil. Increase by seed, division, or stem cuttings.

MEADOW-RUE, TALL (*thalictrum*)
Clusters of white bloom on 10-foot plants from August to September. Give sun or partial shade and well-drained, moist soil. Increase by seed, division, or cuttings.

PARTRIDGEBERRY (*mitchella*)
Small white flowers on plants up to 6 inches tall in June and July. Red berries later. Needs shade and well-drained, moist, and acid soil. Increase with stem cuttings or seed. A good ground cover in shade.

PASQUEFLOWER (*anemone*)
Several species of the anemone tribe are called pasqueflowers. They grow 8 to 16 inches tall with yellow or blue flowers. The yellows are called buttercups. Needs sun and well-drained, dry soil. Increase by seeds or root divisions. An excellent plant for early color.

PHLOX, BLUE (*phlox*)
Pale blue flowers on 6- to 15-inch stems, April and May. Non-flowering part of plant hugs ground. Needs partial shade and well-drained, dry soil. Increase by division or stem cuttings.

POPPY, CALIFORNIA (*eschscholzia*)
Bright orange, cup-like flowers on 10- to 20-inch plants from April to June. Needs sun and well-drained, dry soil. Increase by seeds. Very hardy. Especially beautiful when naturalized in large, open areas.

PRAIRIE ROSE (*rosa*)
Handsome pink flowers in small clusters on spreading branches, up to 15 feet long from May to July. Needs sun and well-drained, dry soil. Increase by seeds or by stem layering.

SAND VERBENA (*abronia*)
Small pink, yellow, or lilac flowers on 12-inch plants from May to September. Likes sun and well-drained soil. Increase by seeds. Trailing stems make it a good ground cover.

SHOOTING STAR (*dodecatheon*)
Small, red-violet blooms in clusters on 1-foot stalks in May to June. Needs partial shade and well-drained, moist soil. Propagate by division, seed, or root cuttings. Disappears in summer.

SPRING-BEAUTY (*claytonia*)
Pinkish-white bloom on 4- to 6-inch plants, March to May. Needs shade and well-drained, dry soil. Increase by division or seeds. Often self-sows.

SUNFLOWER, SAWTOOTH (*helianthus*)
Big yellow bloom with brown centers in clusters on 10-inch plants from July to October. Needs sun, well-drained soil. Increase by seeds or root division.

TRILLIUM (*trillium*)
Showy white or purple bloom on erect terminal stems of 12-inch plants from April to June. Needs shade and moist, well-drained soil. Increase by seeds or root division.

VIOLET, BLUE (*viola*)
Blue flowers on 6- to 8-inch plants from April to June. Needs partial to full shade and well-drained, moist soil. Increase by seed, division, or cuttings.

WOOD ASTER, BLUE (*aster*)
Small, light purple flowers in open clusters in the fall on plants 4 feet tall. Prefers full sun and well-drained, but moist, soil. Increase by division.

HERBS

You'll Love to Grow

Our partnership with nature is never more evident than in our remarkable association with herbs. Part of ancient mythologies, herbs throughout history have been invested with strange and magical powers; in fact, the medicinal qualities of many have been demonstrated time and again. Quinine was extracted from cinchona bark, digitalis from foxglove, and morphine from the opium poppy. Yet the real reason herbs are grown today is for the distinctive flavor they add to many recipes.

Easy to grow, herbs capture the imagination with their sweet or pungent scents. Many are perennials; treat others as annuals and grow them from seed planted each spring. All grow best in full sun. Group all your herbs in a special garden, or tuck those you like best among flowering plants in your sunniest borders. Or as in the garden pictured *opposite*, have a few quick-growing annuals, such as petunia, marigold, and nasturtium mingling delightfully with sage, thyme, oregano, lemon balm, and several varieties of mint. Yarrow and artemesia provide backup color and fragrance along the split-rail fence.

Besides needing sun, most herbs require no special treatment. For help in growing a wide variety of culinary herbs, consult the chart on the following pages.

HERB CHART

Herb	When to Harvest	Comments
Anise	Collect seeds when fully formed. Seed clusters may be snipped into a paper bag. Leaves may be used any time.	Annual. Seed extremely slow to germinate. In northern regions start seed indoors 6 to 8 weeks before last frost.
Bay	Pick mature leaves any time.	Evergreen (tree). Trees will not survive bitter cold winds of northern regions. Grow in container and move indoors in winter. Protect from wind and intense sun.
Basil	Used fresh, leaves may be picked 6 to 8 weeks after planting. For drying, pick leaves just before flowers open.	Annual. Both green and purple-leaved varieties available. Excellent for growing in pots indoors.
Borage	Leaves best when young and tender. Flowers should be picked just as they open, when used for flavoring.	Annual. Particularly attractive blossoms. Usually grown from seed. Needs dry, sunny location.
Caraway	Gather seeds when brown in color.	Biennial. Plants customarily produce seeds the second year.
Catnip	Top leaves and flowers cut and dried when mature.	Perennial. A hardy plant comfortable in sun or shade. Started from seed or root divisions. Pinching back plant encourages bushy growth.
Chervil	Leaves used fresh when fully grown. Pick leaves for drying just before blossoms open.	Annual. Sown from seed in early spring. Likes semi-shade.
Chives	As leaf stalks reach maturity, cut from base of plant.	Perennial. Low-maintenance plants, chives make especially attractive border plants. Will also thrive indoors on sunny windowsill.
Comfrey	Pick young, tender leaves as needed.	Perennial. Prefers moist soil and tolerates partial shade. Pinch back flower heads to force greater leaf growth.
Coriander	Seeds are gathered when fully mature.	Annual. Grown from seed in any good garden soil.
Cress	Pick fully grown leaves for salad or garnish.	Perennial. Water cress requires running water. Other varieties, such as garden cress or winter cress, may be grown in moist soil and partial shade.
Dill	Pick leaves when flower umbels are beginning to open. Seed is gathered when ripe.	Annual. Sown directly in garden from seed as soon as the ground can be worked.
Fennel	Gather seeds when ripe. Stems, picked just before blossoms open, may be eaten like celery.	Perennial. Usually grown as an annual from seed planted in early spring. Prefers sunny location.
Garlic	Dig mature bulbs from ground for sections called "cloves."	Perennial. Will thrive in any good garden soil with ample sunshine. Usually started from sets.
Geranium (scented)	Use leaves any time.	Perennial. Must be wintered indoors in northern regions. Requires full sun but tolerates partial shade. Especially suitable for houseplant.
Horehound	Mature stems and leaves used for flavoring.	Perennial. Weedy growth may have to be contained. Tolerates heat. Grown from seed, cuttings, or divisions.
Lavender	Cut flower spikes as flowers begin to open. Then dry.	Perennial. Thrives in sunny rock gardens but needs well-limed soil. Protect with mulch in regions where winters are severe. May be taken indoors.

Herb	When to Harvest	Comments
Lemon Balm	Pick leaves and sprigs during morning hours.	Perennial. Characterized by weedy growth and may have to be contained. Will grow in poor soil but requires sunny location.
Lemon Verbena	Gather and use leaves when fully mature.	Perennial. Tender shrub plant that must be wintered indoors.
Marjoram	Use fresh leaves at any time.	Perennial. Grown as annual in northern regions.
Mint	Fresh leaves used as they mature. Leaves for drying picked just before flowering begins.	Perennial. Spreading rootstalks can be invasive. Does best in rich, moist soil.
Parsley	Leaves used fresh. Dry on racks in ventilated area. Store in air-tight containers.	Biennial. Usually grown as an annual. Seed germinates slowly. Likes sun but will tolerate partial shade.
Rosemary	Leaves are picked when fully mature.	Perennial. Should be wintered indoors where temperatures are severe.
Sage	Cut leafy tops of stalks and hang in shady, ventilated area until dry.	Perennial. Needs sun and well-drained soil. Cut back occasionally to encourage compact growth.
Summer Savory	Cut tops of plants before flowering and hang for drying.	Annual. Should be started from seed outdoors as soon as the soil can be worked.
Sweet Cicely	Gather seeds when green.	Perennial. Especially attractive for its decorative, fernlike foliage. Prefers partial shade.
Sweet Woodruff	Pick and harvest plants in spring. Then dry.	Perennial. May have to be sheltered indoors if winters are severe. Prefers partial shade.
Tansy	Leaves may be used fresh for subtle, ginger-like flavor. May be poisonous. Use mainly for dried flower arrangements.	Perennial. Rapidly spreading roots may have to be contained. Prefers full sun but will grow in light shade.
Tarragon	Use young leaves and stem tips.	Perennial. Will thrive in partial shade. May need mulch protection in winter.
Thyme	Leafy stalk tips and flower clusters may be dried when blossoms begin to open.	Perennial. Needs well-drained soil and sun. Usually grown from divisions or cuttings.

SPECIAL USES FOR HERBS

Herbs mixed with vegetables can turn a mundane vegetable patch into a showcase of color and texture. An extra benefit is the unusual ability herbs have to repel insects. Planted among beans, marigolds are said to discourage Mexican bean beetles. Nasturtiums can check aphids, striped cucumber beetles, and squash bugs. Tansy planted with cabbage helps reduce cutworms.

Herbs are especially handy when it comes to planting borders or small hedges along walkways or around flower and vegetable beds. Winter savory forms an exquisite low hedge that can be snipped to the desired height. Low-growing thyme, germander, hyssop, and dwarf sage also have compact growth habits that make them ideal for hedges.

A stone outcropping can make a superb background for sweet woodruff, borage, sweet cicely, and various mints.

If a splash of color is needed, plan on a patch or two of marigolds or nasturtiums. Mint, sages, and rosemary offer delicious scents, as well as attractive flowers. Or create a symphony in gray with lamb's ears, santolina, sage, and lavender.

ABCs of Easy-Care Plants

Knowing the needs of the plants you grow is the basis of take-it-easy gardening. All the plants listed on the following 17 pages are easy to grow, even with little care. But if you give a little attention to their specific needs, you will be rewarded with bountiful foliage and bloom. In this section, you'll find the soil, light, and water requirements of many kinds of flowers for your borders, as well as trees and shrubs for your landscape.

Within each category, plants are listed in alphabetical order by common name (unless the botanical name is the only one).

Stately bearded iris are among the loveliest perennial garden plants blooming in May and June.

Annuals

AGERATUM

also called flossflower Almost always in bloom, ageratum adapts well to many soil types; needs full sun to bloom generously.

Fuzzy heads of bloom are usually a blue-violet hue, but there are varieties in white and pink. Dwarfs are 5 to 7 inches tall. Tall types grow to 2 feet high.

Start seed indoors 6 to 8 weeks in advance of last expected frost. Set plants 5 to 9 inches apart. Shorter types are excellent for rock gardens or as an edging for a flower border.

ALYSSUM

sweet alyssum Tiny white, pink, or purple flowers in umbels cover the compact plants from spring to frost. Most will be only 3 or 4 inches tall; a few types extend to 9 or 10 inches.

Full sun is best, but plants will adapt to some shade. Not fussy about type of soil. Sow seed outdoors as soon as soil can be worked, or set out started plants when danger of frost is past.

When setting small plants into the garden, space them 8 to 10 inches apart, because they spread, and each plant will soon cover a fairly large area.

ASTER

(callistephus)
Plants range from 8 inches to 3 feet in height. Flowers may be different: mum, single or double, shaggy or pompon, in many colors. Their centers are often yellow. Choose a sunny or a lightly shaded location. A rich, well-drained soil is best, but you may need to add some lime if your soil is too acidic. Mulch with grass clippings or peat moss to maintain good soil moisture. Start seed early indoors.

BABY'S-BREATH

(gypsophila)
Delicate flowers are scattered on many-branched, 15- to 24-inch stems. Some have flowers that are white, pink, or rose.

Full sun is best, but plants like poor soil. Add lime or wood ashes if your soil is acidic. Sow seed outside as soon as soil has warmed. Transplant, spacing 8 to 12 inches apart. Repeat the sowings every two weeks for a long season of bloom.

BACHELOR'S-BUTTON

(centaurea)
The most common type has blue fringe-petaled flowers that are an old-fashioned favorite. Varieties with pink, white, red, and lavender flowers are easy to find.

Plants average 1 to 3 feet tall, with fine, gray-green foliage. Choose a sunny location. Average soil is fine, if it is well drained. Seeds are hardy. Sow outdoors as soon as ground is workable. Or sow seed in the fall for flowers the following year.

Keep faded flowers snipped off to encourage continuous bloom. Plants show well in massed groupings. Use cut flowers in fresh arrangements.

BEGONIA

wax begonia or fibrous begonia Single or double flowers cover the rounded plants that average 6 to 9 inches in height. Bloom is usually pink, red, or white. Foliage is green, red, or bronze. Plants grow under almost any light conditions and will bloom in shady areas. Soil should be rich and kept moist. Water plants regularly to help them survive hot spells.

Seed is fine and slow to germinate; it's easiest to purchase started plants. Space starts 6 to 8 inches apart. Cuttings root easily.

In late summer, make cuttings to grow indoors in a sunny window for winter bloom. Outdoors, these plants are most effective when used by themselves in a massed bed or as an edging for a shady perennial border.

BELLS-OF-IRELAND

(moluccella)
Spires of green, bell-shaped calyxes growing along the 2- to 3-foot stems explain the name. Tiny white blooms are almost hidden inside.

Average soil is acceptable, but the plant does even better in rich, well-drained soil. Plant in a sunny location and keep evenly moist.

Sow seed outdoors after the danger of frost has passed. Space transplants about 12 inches apart. Use in dried bouquets.

BROWALLIA

Each sprawling plant may cover a 10- to 15-inch square of space. The small, petunia-like flower continues blooming until the first frost. Comes in shades of blue, violet, and white.

Any soil is acceptable, but these plants need to be kept moist. Will grow in full sun or partial shade.

Start seed indoors 6 to 8 weeks before the last frost, or buy starts. Space 8 to 10 inches apart.

BURNING BUSH

(kochia)
Plants are known for their dense, globe-like shapes, formed of tiny lacy leaves. The entire plant turns bright red in fall. Grows 2 to 3 feet tall.

Tolerates heat well and likes full sun. Sow seed outdoors when weather has warmed, or start indoors 4 to 6 weeks earlier. Space 18 to 24 inches apart. Keep soil fairly dry.

CALLIOPSIS

(coreopsis)
Flowers of this annual come in rich shades: golden yellow and mahogany, crimson, maroon, and orange. Dwarfs grow 12 inches high; tall ones to 3 feet.

Sun is the only must for these plants. Sow the seed outdoors as soon as soil can be worked. Thin, so plants are 10 inches apart. Buds and flowers should appear in about 40 days from planting date.

CLEOME

also called spider plant
Cleome blooms from June through August and grows 3 to 6 feet tall. Take your choice of pink, white, or red bloom. Grows in any average soil, if kept fairly dry. Full sun is best; adapts to some shade.

Sow seed outdoors when last frost is past. Thin, so plants will be spaced 18 to 24 inches apart.

COCKSCOMB

(Celosia)
Cockscomb (crested) and plumosa (feathered) are common names of two typical celosias. The names describe the shape of the brilliantly colored flowers in red, orange, pink, and yellow. Blooms are 2 to 12 inches across. Dwarf forms are about 8 inches tall, but taller kinds may reach 18 to 24 inches. Tolerant of all soils but must have full sun to flower.

Start seed indoors 6 to 8 weeks before the last frost is due; space the plants 8 to 12 inches apart.

COLEUS

Colorful foliage is the trademark of these plants, with multicolored patterns of chartreuse, yellow, pink, white, red, and green covering the often ruffled leaves. Insignificant bloom spikes should be pinched off. Plants range from 6 to 24 inches tall.

Plants do best in average to rich, well-drained soil that is not allowed to dry out. Indirect light or partial shade is best. Take cuttings in late summer for indoor winter plants.

COSMOS

Wide, serrated petals in shades of pink, rose, yellow, red, and lavender surround a yellow-gold center of 3- to 4-inch single or double flowers. Grows 4 to 6 feet tall.

Fairly dry, not very rich soil produces earliest bloom. Full sun is best; plants tolerate partial shade. Start seed early indoors. Space plants 12 inches apart.

GLORIOSA DAISY

(rudbeckia)
Hybridized from wild, black-eyed susans, plants are 18 to 36 inches tall and bear daisy-like flowers in shades of yellow, orange, or bronze with a brown center, although one variety has a green center.

Will do well in most soils and will bloom best in full sun. Sow seed outdoors in late fall or early spring. Space young plants 12 to 18 inches apart. Plants should be kept trimmed to encourage the longest season of continuous bloom. Flowers are long-lasting in cut arrangements.

GLOBE AMARANTH

(gomphrena)
Mounded plants, 6 to 24 inches tall, are continuously covered with ¾-inch, clover-like bloom in red, pink, yellow, purple, and white. Plants do well in any type of soil but need full sun.

Germination takes 12 to 14 days, so start seed indoors 6 to 8 weeks before the last expected frost. Set plants 8 to 12 inches apart.

Good for dried bouquets. Cut when fully open; hang heads down to dry.

HOLLYHOCK

(alcea)
This old favorite sends up 2- to 6-foot spikes of bloom that may be single, double, or frilled. Bloom is 3 to 4 inches wide. Colors include red, rose, pink, and yellow. Plants do best in full sun but are not fussy about soil type. Start seed indoors 6 to 8 weeks before last frost is due; set outside when night temperatures warm. Space 12 to 24 inches apart.

Natives of the Orient, hollyhocks can be annuals, biennials, or perennials, depending on variety

and location. Grow them along fences and walls, or use them as attractive backdrops for flower beds.

IMPATIENS

sultana
These compact plants—usually 6 to 18 inches tall—mound to cover a wide area. Flat bloom looks like violets and appears all over plants in shades of pink, red, purple, white, and orange, plus some bicolors.

Buy started plants to set outdoors after weather warms, or sow seed indoors 6 to 8 weeks before the last expected frost. Cuttings root easily. Partial shade is preferable.

LANTANA

Available in both bush and trailing types. Common lantana is about 3 feet tall; dwarf varieties 12 to 18 inches. Clusters of tiny flowers are pink, yellow, white, red, or bronze.

Both varieties prefer rich, well-drained soil and full sun but will tolerate partial shade. Seed is slow to germinate, so buy young plants. Space 12 to 18 inches apart.

LARKSPUR

(consolida)
Known and loved for its spikes of blue bloom, larkspur also comes in shades of rose or white. Plants can either be branched or hyacinth-like—with one big flowering stalk. A common type is usually 3 to 5 feet tall, but a dwarf variety only 12 inches tall is also available. Larkspur prefers a light, well-drained fertile soil but adapts to other types. Full sun is best, though the plant needs some shade in hot climates. Sow seed outdoors in late fall or early spring.

LOBELIA

There are compact and trailing varieties of lobelias. Compact varieties grow 6 inches tall and are covered with ½-inch flowers of blue, white, pink, or lavender. Trailing varieties grow up to 2 feet.

Give plants full sun and rich, moist soil. Where summers are hot, plants require some shade. Set compact varieties 6 inches apart.

MARIGOLD
(tagetes)

This easiest-to-grow annual has many forms and a range of colors, including bright orange, yellow, and, recently, white and cream. Foliage is a deep green and finely cut. Most have a pungent scent, although this has been bred out of newer varieties.

Full sun is the only requirement. Sow seed outdoors after last frost, or start indoors 6 weeks earlier. Started seedlings are readily available. Space plants 6 to 12 inches apart, depending on variety.

MOSS ROSE
(portulaca)

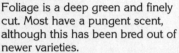

Spreads a carpet of bright-colored bloom on poor, dry soil. Dark-green foliage is needle-like. Plants range from 3 to 6 inches tall. Full sun and well-drained soil are necessary for good bloom. Seed is fine and may be mixed with sand to get even coverage. Sow outdoors after ground warms. Plant self-sows but color is less vivid second year. Sow fresh seed each year.

NASTURTIUM
(tropaeolum)

Flowers come in shades of red, yellow, pink, and white. Bush varieties are 8 to 15 inches tall; climbing types may reach 6 feet. Flowers are single or double.

Seedlings are hard to transplant, so sow outdoors after last frost. Thin bush types to 6 inches, and climbers to 10 inches. Nasturtiums thrive on neglect, including poor soil and little water.

PANSY
(viola sp.)

Face-like markings on large, open flowers characterize this sentimental favorite. Plants average about 8 inches in height and tend to spread out. Many colors and varieties.

Sow seed outdoors in fall; move to a cold frame for winter months and set into garden locations as early as ground can be worked. Started plants are widely available.

PERIWINKLE
(vinca)

The annual form of vinca is a bushy plant, 1 to 2 feet tall, with shiny green leaves and five-petaled open bloom in shades of blue, pink, and white. The plant prefers full sun, if soil is kept moist. In hot areas, some shade is needed. Sow seed indoors 3 months before last frost is due. Space 8 to 10 inches apart.

PETUNIA

Colors, shapes, and sizes of this popular annual vary widely. One major type is classified as multiflora. It produces many 2- to 3-inch single or double blooms. Many gardeners find this the easiest type to grow.

A second type is grandiflora. These plants bear flowers measuring up to 5 inches across. Often, they're ruffled and fringed. Petunias are available in both bush and trailing varieties. The latter can be used in hanging baskets.

PINKS
(dianthus)

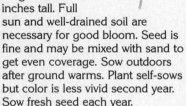

The annual form of dianthus has popular varieties, including those that bear bloom of pink, white, red, and bicolors. They may be single or double. Plants range from 8 to 12 inches in height. Full sun and a light, well-drained soil will give good results. Add lime or wood ash if the soil is acidic. Sow seed outdoors after the last frost. Space seedlings 8 inches apart. A great choice for edging a flower border.

SALVIA

Spikes of red bloom characterize this popular annual. Plants are usually 12 to 30 inches tall; dwarfs, from 6 to 10 inches. Needs full sun for at least a half day and rich, well-drained soil. The seed is hard to germinate; it's easier to buy starts. Space 12 inches apart.

SNAPDRAGON
(antirrhinum)

Plants range from 7-inch dwarfs to 3-foot giants. Rainbow hues and single or double forms add variety. Plants need rich, well-drained soil and nearly full sun. Start seed indoors 8 weeks before last frost, or buy started plants. Set out as soon as the ground's workable.

SWEET WILLIAM
(dianthus)

An old-fashioned favorite in the dianthus family, this compact plant may be as short as 4 inches or as tall as 2 feet. Bloom is in flat clusters of red, purple, pink, and whites. Full sun and moist, light soil are best. Buy started plants, or sow seed indoors 7 weeks before the last expected frost. Space plants 8 to 10 inches apart in the garden.

VERBENA

Creeping and upright types available. Flowers are fragrant and of many colors. Heights: 6 to 15 inches. Sow seed in garden after the last frost.

ZINNIA

Tallest kinds may be 3 to 4 feet tall; dwarfs only 6 to 12 inches. Flower petals may be wide, fringed, shaggy, or pointed and solid, or bicolored. Zinnias like hot weather and full sun. They adapt to any soil. Sow seed outdoors when temperatures warm. Space the seedlings from 6 to 12 inches apart, depending on whether you're growing dwarfs or taller varieties. You can expect a lot of color and few problems with this easy-to-grow annual. Plant several kinds.

65

Perennials

ALYSSUM

(Aurinia saxatilis)
Hardy from Zone
3 southward. This
spring-blooming
plant is not the
annual known as
"sweet alyssum."
It's also called
"basket-of-gold,"

and its plentiful yellow bloom makes
it a good companion for spring
bulbs. It prefers full sun but adjusts
to partial sun. Ordinary garden soil is
acceptable.

A. saxatilis 'citrina' is the most
floriferous variety; A. saxatilis
compacta has somewhat shorter
stems than 'citrina,' which grows 12
to 15 inches tall but otherwise has
similar growth habits.

Both varieties listed can be easily
propagated by means of seed, stem
cuttings, or root division.

ASTER

also called michaelmas daisy
This plant, in some varieties, grows
to 48 inches in height. Most bloom
in late summer or early fall.

Hardy asters need no more than
adequate sun and water to produce
important late bloom. Among the
best-loved of the many varieties
available are Harrington's Pink,
Sailor Boy (violet with yellow eyes),
and Boningale White. One of the
good dwarfs of the tribe is Jenny,
15 inches tall with cyclamen-
red flowers.

Plants should be lifted, divided,
and replanted every three years.

ASTILBE

also called false spirea
This handsome plant is the answer
for many gardeners who want color
in shade. It's hardy from Zone 4
south, grows 15 to 30 inches tall,
depending on variety, and blooms in
June or July. Increase your supply by
root division in early spring or in
the fall.

Available in shades of pink, white,
red, and salmon, astilbes prefer a
damp location. They're hardy
enough to use as a ground cover in
shady spots and will provide
welcome color at mid-border
locations in mixed borders.

BABY'S-BREATH

(Gypsophila paniculata)
Hardy from Zone 3 south, it grows to
4 feet tall and prefers full sun. It can
be propagated by root cuttings in
midsummer.

Perennial baby's-breath needs a
well-drained, alkaline soil and lots of
space to perform at its best.
Because plants grow almost as
wide as they are tall, set new plants
about 6 feet apart in a permanent
location. Their tap roots make it
almost impossible to move large
plants successfully.

Stake securely, so wind and rain
won't send them sprawling over
their immediate neighbors in a
mixed border. They dry well and
make good fall arrangements.

BALLOON FLOWER

*(Platycodon
grandiflorus)*
Hardy from Zone
3 south, it's about
20 inches in
height and comes
in blue, pink, and
white varieties. All
bloom in July and

August, and all require full sun. Most
popular in its blue form, this hardy
perennial takes a year or two to
become well established, then goes
on to bloom for years.

Its common name describes buds
that are round and puffy before they
open, resembling tiny balloons. The
fleshy, tuber-like roots should be
planted so crowns are just below soil
level, with at least a foot of space
between each plant. Don't move
them once they're established.

Start from seed sown in late
summer. Transplant to a cold frame
for winter. Move to garden when
danger of frost has passed.

BEEBALM

(Monarda didyma); also known as
bergamot
This plant is hardy from Zone 4
south. It grows 2 to 3 feet tall and
comes in pink, red, purple, and
white varieties. All bloom in July and
August, and all varieties prefer full
sun but will adapt to partial sun.
Increase plants by root division in
the spring.

Beebalm is attractive to bees
and also to hummingbirds. It is a
valuable mid-border plant; extremely
hardy, it withstands drought and
heat.

Even when not in bloom, it is easy
to recognize from its square-shaped
stem—a characteristic of plants
belonging to the mint tribe. The wild
variety, with lavender bloom, is, in
fact, called "horse mint."

Beebalm performs well even in
sandy or heavy soil. Clumps
increase in size rapidly.

BELLFLOWER

(Campanula sp.)
This large species includes varieties
as short as 8 inches and as tall as 36
inches. Flower colors are blue and
white, appearing in June.

Sun or light shade is acceptable.
Root division should be done in
early spring. Some varieties are
hardy from Zone 3 south; others, not
farther north than Zone 5. All
varieties need winter protection.

BLEEDING HEART

(Dicentra spectabilis)
Hardy from Zone
4 south, it grows
up to 24 inches
high and blooms
in early spring.
Has pink,
heart-shaped
flowers. Set new
plants 24 inches

apart to make room for their arching
stems. When set close to flowering
spring bulbs and annual or
perennial (anchusa) forget-me-nots,
bleeding heart has endearing
charm.

As summer progresses, foliage is
prone to die back. For this reason,
mark the location with a stake to
avoid disturbing roots if you plan to
overplant barren areas with annuals
for summer color.

Bleeding heart may be grown
from seed sown in late summer,
wintered in a cold frame, then
moved to the border when the
danger of frost is past.

In fact, allow some bloom to go to
seed, saving it in case the mother
plant fails to emerge after a fall and
winter of adverse weather.

BUTTERFLY WEED
(*Asclepias tuberosa*)
Flowers appear from July to September, with bright orange umbels of bloom on stems 2 to 3 feet tall. It needs full sun but is not fussy about soil. Hardy from Zone 5 southward, this colorful plant is often found growing wild, but it is readily available from commercial plantsmen. Slow to come up in spring; use marker to locate.

CANDYTUFT
(*Iberis sempervirens*)
Hardy from Zone 3 south. White bloom in May on stems 4 to 8 inches tall. It needs full sun to do its best. Foliage is evergreen in mild climates; dies down where winters are severe.

Plants are easily propagated by seed, stem cuttings, or division. If soil is poor, add compost and coarse sand. Good underplanting for May tulips.

CHRYSANTHEMUM
(*Chrysanthe-mum* sp.)
The hardy chrysanthemum is one of the joys of the autumn garden. Endless varieties put splashes of gold,

white, red, bronze, or purple in the fall scene. Depending on the variety, they are hardy from Zone 3 south. In northern zones, pick the kinds that bloom early to make certain the bloom won't be killed by frost.

Major divisions of the flower generally called chrysanthemum are: cushion, decorative, pompon, spider, and spoon.

For most, the length of the day determines when they bloom. They bloom when days grow shorter. In short-season areas, use locally grown varieties to insure bloom.

In spring, lift plants and divide, discarding dead centers; replant the divisions 8 to 12 inches apart.

Feverfew, also a member of this big family, is hardy from Zone 3 south and blooms on 30-inch stems in midsummer, requiring sun or partial sun.

COLUMBINE
(*Aquilegia* sp.)
It's been hybridized to produce a fine group of hardy perennials in red, blue, white, pink, and yellow. June is the major bloom season.

Hardy from Zone 3 south. Full sun is best. The native plant, from which the McKana hybrid strain has been developed, has red sepals and yellow spurs on 12- to 24-inch stalks. Heights of hybrid varieties may vary from 24 to 30 inches.

When the flowering period ends, cut foliage back to about 4 inches.

CORALBELLS
(*Heuchera sanguinea*); also called alumroot
It is hardy from Zone 3 south. Flower colors include white, pink, red, and chartreuse. Bloom period extends from June to September. These plants need sun or partial sun. Foliage grows in mounds even when plant is not in bloom. Leaf mound is about 8 inches high, but the flower stems grow 18 inches tall.

DAYLILIES
(*Hemerocallis* sp.)
The Greek name for this plant means "beautiful for a day." Indeed, each flower remains open for only one day, but

each stem has dozens of buds that continue to open for weeks. Hardy from Zone 2 south, this plant is nearly trouble free. It's available in yellows, oranges, pinks, and reds. Depending on variety, bloom periods begin in early summer and continue into late September. Growers list plants as early, mid-season, and late.

Set new plants a foot apart. You can divide and reset divisions at any time of the year, though early spring is the best. Plants need no special soil but will flower more freely if you fertilize them in fall or spring.

DELPHINIUM
Plants of this species are hardy from Zone 3 south. Depending on variety, they may be as tall as 6 to 8 feet, with bloom colors including white, blue, yellow, pink, and lavender.

Start with sturdy nursery plants in spring. Impressive hybrid varieties include the famous Round Table series of Pacific Coast hybrids and the English Blackmore and Langdon hybrids. Plants need full sun and fertile soil to perform well. Space new plants 2 feet apart, and stake at planting time.

GAILLARDIA
also known as the blanket flower
The plant is hardy from Zone 3 south. Flowers are available in shades of gold, red, and orange. Summer is the bloom period. Full sun's needed for best

performance. There is also an annual called gaillardia.

Hybrid perennials make fine border plants, with bloom as much as 3 inches across on 30-inch stems. If the plant doesn't send up new foliage in spring, don't discard it. Dig up, divide, and replant divisions, spacing 12 inches apart.

GASPLANT
(*Dictamnus* sp.)
On a hot night when no breezes are stirring, you can often get a small burst of flame by holding a lighted match over the bloom of this plant. Hence, the common name.

Hardy from Zone 3 south, plants grow 1½ to 2½ feet tall. They need full sun. Flower colors are white or pink, appearing in summer.

Once established, plants are very hard to move, so try to set into a permanent position. You can grow this plant from seed, but it's not easy to do. You'll probably have best luck if you purchase started plants.

Plant close to late-blooming spuria iris for a handsome effect. Foliage remains atractive when bloom's gone.

67

GLOBEFLOWER

(Trollius europaeus)
Blooms in May and June; is hardy from Zone 3 south. May be 30 inches tall. Flowers are yellow or orange. Partial shade is best. Large ball-shaped bloom on tall sturdy stems makes this a desirable plant if you can offer the moist and partly shaded location it needs. When planting, spade in lots of humus and mulch well to hold in soil moisture. Space plants 8 to 10 inches from each other.

GLOBE THISTLE

(Echinops exaltatus)
Hardy from Zone 4 south, it reaches 4 feet in height and flowers in July with blue bloom and silvery foliage. It needs sun or partial sun to bloom well. An easy plant to propagate from seed or by division.

Don't confuse this desirable plant with the farmer's pest, the Canadian thistle. Use for back-of-the-border placement. Taplow Blue variety is a perfect foil for yellow daylilies.

HOSTA

also known as the plantain lily and funkia
These plants are grown primarily for their lovely foliage and for their ability to put fresh beauty into a shaded garden location. Hardy from Zone 3 south. Heights range from dwarf to 30 inches. Flowers borne on tall stems arise from rosettes of foliage and may be white, blue, violet, or lilac. July and August are major periods of bloom.

IRIS

This genus includes such diverse varieties that it is not easy to generalize about them. However, most are hardy from Zone 3 south. Bloom colors include white, blue, violet-purple, yellow, orange, red, rose, and pink. Sizes range from dwarf up to 38 inches. Bloom periods vary from spring through summer, depending on variety. There are bulbous, tuberous, and rhizomatous kinds. Major classes include bulbous, tall bearded, dwarf bearded, Dutch, Japanese, Siberian, and spuria.

Among the rhizomatous kinds, tall bearded iris are reasonably perennial in Zone 3 with winter protection; but, more dependably so in Zones 4 to 8. Lift, divide, and replant all kinds about once every three years. Give full sun and a well-drained, lean soil.

LOOSESTRIFE

(Lythrum sp.)
One of the most popular is the vivid purple Dropmore, which blooms constantly all summer. Twenty- to 36-inch flower spikes make it good for mid- or back-border placement. Hardy from Zone 3 south. Colors available include pink, red, and purple. The plants need full or partial sun and do best in moist soil.

LUPINE

If you live where summers are long and hot, lupines are not for you. Hardy from Zone 3 south, they grow from 3 to 5 feet tall, with flowers in a range of colors, including blue, pink, red, yellow, purple, and bicolors. They need full sun and bloom for long periods of time—from spring into summer in mild climates. Buy started plants because it takes two years to grow from seed to bloom.

PAINTED DAISY

also known as pyrethrum
These plants are members of the chrysanthemum family. Hardy from Zone 4 south, they bloom in June and July at heights of 14 to 24 inches. Flowers may be red, white, or pink.

Fernlike foliage and colorful flowers make this a desirable mixed border plant. When setting out new plants, space them a foot apart. Each clump will increase in size and after 2 or 3 years may be lifted, divided, and replanted to increase your store. The best time to do this is late summer.

Painted daisies need a rich soil and ample moisture. If your soil is poor, prepare the bed in advance by spading in compost, leaf mold, or well-rotted cow manure. Water the location thoroughly, and let stand for several days before setting plants in place.

PENSTEMON

Hardy from Zones 3 to 5 southward, depending on variety, these plants are from 12 to 20 inches tall, with bloom in shades of blue, purple, red, and rose. Sun or light shade is best; if drainage is good and plants have ample water, they will grow in almost any garden soil. Flowers are reminiscent of foxglove in shape, with many blooms on each stem. They're a good flower for cutting, and the spiky form recommends them for mixed border plantings to contrast plants that have rounded bloom. Plant in spring or fall; space 10 inches apart.

One recommended variety, Firebird, has ruby blooms on 18- to 24-inch stems. It's free from pests and free-flowering. Zone 5.

PEONY

(Paeonia sp.)
Includes single and double types, Japanese, tree, and spuria varieties with colors of white, red, pink, and yellow occurring in tree peonies. All bloom in May and June.

Hardy from Zone 3 south; heights range from 18 to 30 inches. All varieties perform best in sun. To propagate herbaceous types, divide roots in fall. Do *not* prune back tree peonies except to remove dead parts and the bloom stem, once bloom is spent.

Double herbaceous peonies are a major early summer event in most parts of the country. Huge blooms and attractive foliage are endearing qualities. So are resistance to pests, long life, and an ability to withstand drought and hot summer weather.

Among herbaceous types, there are early-, mid-, and late-season kinds. Choose some of each to prolong the season of bloom.

PHLOX

This species provides fragrant tresses of colorful, long-lasting bloom from July until the first frost. Hardy from Zone 4 south, phlox grows up to 4 feet tall. It needs sun or partial sun and rich soil to perform well. If your soil is poor, spade in bone meal or other plant food. Space plants a foot apart in a well-drained location.

Bloom colors include white, red, pink, lavender, and purple. The most important work in hybridizing phlox has been done by the late Captain Symons-Jeune. Many varieties created by him have brilliant "eyes" of color that contrast with the main color of the florets.

PINKS

(*Dianthus* sp.)
Includes hardy varieties in Zones 3 to 7. Heights vary from 3 to 24 inches and flower colors from pink to red and white.

All bloom in summer, and all need full or partial sun if they are to bloom freely. You can propagate pinks from seed, cuttings, or by root division. Use the latter method in early spring. Set new plants 4 to 12 inches apart, depending on their mature height. In acidic soil, add lime to make it more alkaline.

POPPY

(*Papaver orientale*)
also called Oriental poppy
Hardy from Zone 2 south. Height varies from 2 to 4 feet, depending on variety. Bloom colors include red, white, pink, orange, and lavender. All varieties bloom in early summer. Today's hybrids, developed

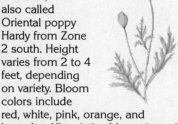

from varieties that grow wild in Mediterranean countries, are dazzlingly large and colorful. Flower heads often measure 6 to 8 inches across, with soft, gleaming petals reminiscent of the finest silk cloth.

Poppies perform best in rich loam. New plants must be set out in August or September, when plants are dormant. Space 15 to 18 inches apart, and place crown 2 inches below soil level.

RUDBECKIA

also known as coneflower
This plant is hardy from Zone 3 south. Can grow up to 30 inches. Plants are in flower from July until the first frost.

They need at least partial sun but will grow in any average soil. Close relatives are black- or brown-eyed susans. Two cultivated varieties of rudbeckia can and should be grown in almost any mixed border. They are Gold Drop and Goldsturm. Both produce large, golden-yellow flowers when few other perennials are in bloom. Gold Drop is double; Goldsturm, single.

SEDUM

also called stonecrop
This large genus includes dwarfs and plants up to 2 feet in height. All are hardy from Zone 3 south. Flower colors include orange, yellow, red, pink, cream, white, and rust-brown. Periods of bloom are spring to late summer. Fleshy leaves enable plants to withstand drought.

STOKESIA

also called 'Stokes' aster
These plants are hardy from Zone 5 south. Heights range from 12 to 15 inches. Flowers are light blue or white, blooming July to September. They require a sunny location. A valuable midsummer-

into-autumn bloomer in the perennial border. It needs sun and good drainage, but otherwise stokesia is undemanding. Plant in early spring or in autumn, spacing 6 inches apart. Blue Danube is the most widely grown variety; flowers measure up to 5 inches wide.

THRIFT

(*Armeria maritima*); also called sea thrift and sea pink
Hardy from Zone 3 south. A dwarf, with flowers in rose or white, blooming from May to July. Plant needs full sun but grows in any type of soil. Set out new plants in spring or autumn; space about 8 inches apart. Each will soon form a tidy mound of foliage from which bloom stems arise.

YARROW

(*Achillea* sp.)
Hardy from Zone 3 south. Height varies from 6 inches to 3 feet. Bloom colors are white, red, and yellow. Periods of bloom range from

June to September. Most are tall—2 to 3 feet. Some are excellent to cut, dry, and use in autumn arrangements—Coronation Gold, for example. It grows 3 feet tall. Plants do well in dry locations. If your soil's acidic, add lime to make it more alkaline. Increase number by root division of large clumps.

YUCCA

Hardy from Zone 4 south, these plants form impressive balls of sword-like foliage up to 3 feet in height. They prefer a sunny, hot, dry location. Yuccas put on their show of bloom in spectacular fashion, sending up bloom spikes as high as 6 feet, with half the length covered by bell-shaped flowers of creamy white. If you can supply good drainage, you should have no trouble growing yuccas.

Yucca filamentosa Bright Edge, one of the newer varieties, carries a band of gold edging on deep green, spiky leaves.

69

Tender Bulbs

BEGONIA, TUBEROUS
(Begonia x. tuberosa)
Many varieties of this gorgeously flowered plant— single, double, and pendulant— make it a favorite summer-flowering plant in lightly  shaded areas. Start them indoors by mid-April in a moist mixture of peat moss and vermiculite. Cover tubers with a half inch of starting medium. Move outdoors and fertilize monthly when the danger of frost has passed. Water regularly.

After first frost, dig tubers for winter storage. See pages 36 and 37 for more detailed information on how to do this.

CALADIUM
(Caladium x hortulanum)
Fancy-leaved caladiums will perform in light shade, supplying color all summer long. Handle planting as for tuberous begonias. Plant bulbs 3 inches deep when setting outdoors. Space 8 to 12 inches apart in fairly rich soil. When foliage dies back at first frost, bulbs should be dug and stored indoors.

CALLA LILY
(Zantedeschia aetiopica)
Calla lilies are hardy from Zone 7 southward. In the northern zones, start indoors as for tuberous begonias. When setting outdoors, choose a sunny location in soil enriched with well-rotted cow manure. During the growing season, keep plants moist and well fed. Store in winter as for begonias.

DAHLIA
(Dahlia sp.)
This lovely and widely varied summer-blooming plant may be grown from seed or from tubers. Dahlias do well in either acid or alkaline soil. Types vary from dwarf bedding plants to six-footers. Give ample sun, water, and food.

Plant outdoors after last expected frost, spacing tubers of dwarfs 18 inches apart, giants 3 feet apart. Plant tubers horizontally about 6 inches deep. Drive in sturdy stakes near tubers at planting time. Heavy tops and big flowers will need support later on. Store over winter, following instructions for tuberous begonias.

GLADIOLUS
(Gladiolus x hortulanus)
Two-inch corms produce the best bloom. Always dust lightly with an insecticide-fungicide before you plant them. They don't adapt well to the mixed border because they need staking if their stems are weak. Plant in open, sunny location, spacing rows about 20 inches apart and corms 6 inches deep, 6 inches apart. Water well in dry spells. Dig corms and store for winter in open containers at 40 to 50 degrees (Fahrenheit).

GLORIOSA LILY
(Gloriosa rothchildiana)
Easy to grow as a pot plant or to set into the garden. Start as for tuberous begonias. If you move it to the garden, provide a trellis support. Choose a sunny location; water well during the summer, withholding water in fall. Dig and store for winter as for dahlias, or lift entire plant and set into a pot. Grown in a sunny window, it provides beautiful bloom during the winter.

LILY-OF-THE-NILE
(Agapanthus africanus)
Agapanthus are relatives of the lily, with blue bloom in summer. Plant in large pots with good drainage at the bottom and with a 2- to 3-inch layer of gravel. Fill the container with a mixture of two parts loam and one part each of well-rotted cow manure and sand. Cover bulbs with an inch of potting mix. Water and feed regularly. You seldom get bloom until plant is potbound. After frost, store indoors in cool, dim spot. Water once a month.

PERUVIAN DAFFODIL
(Hymenocallis narcissiflora)
Hymenocallis or the Peruvian daffodil belongs to the amaryllis family. It is not hardy north of Zone 6. A native variety is often bedded out from Kentucky southward. All have white bloom and strap foliage.

Grow in sun in rich soil, planting after soil warms. After frost, lift and store as for tuberous begonias.

TIGRIDIA
(Tigridia pavonia)
Also called tiger flower or Mexican shell-flower, these corms are handled as gladiolus. The bloom colors may  be scarlet, rose, yellow, orange, pink, or white. The mature plant reaches a height of 2 feet. Winter-hardy as far north as Zone 5 (with winter mulch). Grow in rich, well-drained soil in a spot that receives all but midday sun. In North, store corms for winter as for gladiolus.

TUBEROSE
(Polianthes tuberosa)
These fragrant members of the amaryllis tribe are easy to grow in rich garden soil and a sunny location. Plant outdoors after all danger of frost has passed, spacing 6 inches apart. Cover with 2 inches of soil. Keep moist while growing and feed regularly with liquid fertilizer. Stagger planting dates for a longer season of bloom. After frost, lift, let dry, cut back tops, and store in crates indoors, soil attached.

ZEPHYR-LILY
(Zephyranthes sp.)
The variety *Z. candida* is hardy as far north as Zone 5 with winter protection. In northern zones, start indoors in April in shallow clay pots in a mixture of two parts garden soil to one part each peat moss and coarse sand. Funnel-shaped flowers—white, red, yellow, pink, bronze—appear mostly in late summer and early fall. Plant only 1 inch deep. Dig before frost and store in a cool basement.

Hardy Bulbs

CROCUS
(Crocus sp.)

Brilliant colors of crocus flowers announce spring, sometimes blooming through the snow. Plant 4 inches deep, 2 to 3 inches apart. They reappear year after year, increasing by offsets. Species crocus bloom earlier than hybrids. Plant some of both kinds for a long season of bloom. For an eye-catching effect, plant crocus in beds of ground cover, such as ajuga or vinca minor.

DAFFODIL
(Narcissus sp.)
The large narcissus family includes trumpet varieties that are often called daffodils. Plant in groups in the flower border, or naturalize in informal areas. Plant bulbs 8 to 9 inches deep and 4 to 5 inches apart. All varieties should be set in the ground in fall. Put a handful of bone meal in the bottom of each hole. Be sure location is well drained; all bulbs are subject to rot if water stands where they're planted. Fertilize each spring after bloom period has ended.

GRAPE HYACINTH
(Muscari sp.)
Vivid spikes of blue flowers make this a most striking addition to spring gardens when planted in a mass. Set bulbs 4 inches deep, and space them from 2 to 3 inches apart. Although there is a white variety available, the blue grape hyacinth is better known. Culture of grape hyacinths is, in general, the same as described for daffodils, *above,* except for differences in depth of planting and spacing of bulbs.

HYACINTH
(Hyacinthus orientalis)
Hyacinths perfume the air of a spring bulb garden and add their bright colors of blue-purple, rose-pink, white, and yellow. One of the larger of the spring-flowering bulbs, hyacinths need to be planted about 8 inches deep and spaced from 4 to 6 inches apart.

LILY
(Lilium sp.)
The genus lilium is so large it's difficult to generalize about culture. But, in general, all the lilies should be planted from 4 to 8 inches deep, except the martagons and madonnas; these should be covered by no more than 2 inches and an inch of soil, respectively. Mulch around the base of lilies to keep the roots cool. Good drainage is also a must. Lilies are never truly dormant and should be planted promptly after purchase.

RESURRECTION LILY
(Lycoris squamigera)
Plant this hardy, summer-flowering amaryllis in the fall. Set bulbs 5 or 6 inches deep; space 6 to 8 inches apart in well-drained spot. In early spring, green foliage appears. This dies down in early summer, and in August flower stalks spring up to a height of 2 to 3 feet, topped by umbels of lily-shaped bloom in a soft, lavender-pink hue. Use in flower arrangements.

SCILLA
(Scilla sp.)
Most varieties do well even in shade, although flowers are more abundant in sun. Flowering stalks are 18 to 20 inches tall; leaves are grasslike.
   Hardy from Zone 4 southward, bulbs must be planted in the fall. Set them 4 inches deep and 3 to 4 inches apart. Flower colors available are blue, pink, and white.

SNOWDROP
(Galanthus sp.)
Snowdrops present nodding, white, bell-shaped blooms, often before the ground is free of frost. Plant them 3 inches deep and 3 inches apart in light shade. Hardy from Zone 4 south, they are inexpensive and will multiply quickly if you are careful to let foliage ripen naturally. They prefer a rich, well-drained soil. Dig in compost if your soil is poor or too compact.

SQUILL
(Scilla siberica)
The blue squill will bloom very early if planted in a sunny location. Set bulbs about 3 inches deep, and space 3 to 4 inches apart.
   Nodding, blue bells on 4- to 6-inch stems are one of springtime's finest sights, especially when mass planted. Good drainage is necessary for all bulbs if they are to survive and multiply in numbers. Let foliage yellow and ripen off naturally.

TULIP
(Tulipa sp.)

Because tulips form such a varied tribe, they deserve a place in every garden. Consult bulb catalogs to find species or botanical types. They're closer to being perennials than are darwin or cottage types. Included in the group are fosteriana, greigi, and kaufmanniana tulips. Bunch-flowered tulips send up several blooms on a branched stem. In the May-flowering group are cottage and darwins. Don't overlook the lily-flowered, parrot, peony, and fringed tulips. All must have excellent drainage and full sun in spring. Let foliage ripen naturally, helping bulbs form next spring's bloom. Fertilize each spring following the season of bloom. Plant 5 inches deep, and space bulbs 4 to 6 inches apart. Include several kinds of tulips for an extended season of bloom and variety of flower forms.

Trees

ASH
(Fraxinus sp.)
Included are a great many trees grown primarily for shade. *Fraxinus americana,* or the white ash, is 120 feet tall at maturity and is hardy  from Zones 5 to 8. It leafs out late and sheds foliage early in autumn. This variety has shallow roots, so plant sparingly beneath it or there will be too much competition for soil nutrients.

F. pennsylvanica, or green ash, is similar in growth habits to the white ash but is even hardier—Zones 3 to 9.

F. quadrangulata, or blue ash, is hardy from Zones 4 to 9. Mature height is 60 feet.

ASPEN
(Populus sp.)
The populus genus is one of the biggest of tree families, including many kinds of poplar, aspen, and cottonwood.

Populus tremuloides, the quaking aspen, is a small tree with small, round leaves, pointed at the tip, borne on long stems so that every breeze causes the leaves to flutter. Bark of young trees is gray-white. It is found in wooded areas of the far north and in mountainous areas as far south as Mexico.

BUCKEYE
(Aesculus sp.)
Aesculus hippocastanum 'baumanni,' the Baumann horse chestnut, bears double white bloom in spring but does not bear fruit. It is hardy from Zones 3 to 9. *A. glabra,* the Ohio Buckeye, hardy from Zones 5 to 8, is a tree of rounded form, reaching a mature height of about 30 feet. It has greenish-yellow flowers in spring. Foliage turns red-orange in autumn.

A. carnea, the Red Horse Chestnut, grows to a mature height of 40 feet or more and is hardy from Zones 4 to 9. Spring bloom is of a deep rose color.

BIRCH, RIVER
(Betula sp.)
Betula nigra, or river birch, grows 60 to 80 feet tall at maturity. It needs ample moisture and has somewhat shaggy bark, unlike the popular canoe or paper birch. The river birch is a preferred species because it is not subject to the birch-bark borers that have all but eliminated the paper birch, except in far northern zones. Many kinds of birds use its dense foliage to nest in. It's hardy from Massachusetts to Florida and west to Kansas and Minnesota.

CHERRY
(Prunus sp.)
Within the prunus species are different kinds of flowering or oriental cherries that highlight a spring garden when laden with 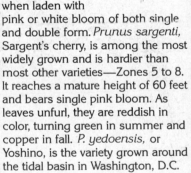 pink or white bloom of both single and double form. *Prunus sargenti,* Sargent's cherry, is among the most widely grown and is hardier than most other varieties—Zones 5 to 8. It reaches a mature height of 60 feet and bears single pink bloom. As leaves unfurl, they are reddish in color, turning green in summer and copper in fall. *P. yedoensis,* or Yoshino, is the variety grown around the tidal basin in Washington, D.C.

CRAB APPLE
(Pyrus sp.)
Pyrus, the botanical name for crabs, includes a number of small-fruited varieties that are exceptionally decorative ornamental trees when covered with spring bloom. One of the most widely grown and loved is the Sargent crab apple. Growing to a height of 8 feet, it's one of the smallest of the flowering crab apple varieties, but it does need considerable space to accommodate its wide branches—up to 15 feet. Fruits are smaller than those of most crab apples; they turn red earlier in fall and remain on the tree, attracting birds. Zone 5.

DOGWOOD
(Cornus sp.)
The cornus genus gives us some of the most graceful ornamental trees and shrubs in or out of bloom.

Cornus florida is one of America's favorite varieties. It's hardy from Zones 5 to 9. Pure white, four-petaled bracts are followed in autumn by bright red fruits. Foliage takes on handsome fall coloring. Varieties within this group include pink, red, and double-flowered kinds, as well as weeping forms. Mature height is about 40 feet.

C. alternifolia, or Pagoda Dogwood, is hardy from Zones 2 to 9. It reaches a mature height of no more than 15 feet. When growing this as a tree rather than a shrub, cut away all but a single trunk.

GINGKO
(Gingko biloba)
The maidenhair tree is the last survivor of a once numerous tribe. Today, its durability is proved by an ability to survive in the highly polluted air of some urban areas. Leathery, fan-shaped leaves are unique. Plant only a grafted male tree; females have a noxious odor. Hardy Zones 5 to 9.

HAWTHORN
(Crataegus sp.)
Hawthorn is valued for white bloom in spring, glossy foliage in summer, orange to scarlet foliage in autumn, and  bright red fruits in fall. Mature height varies, but some species will reach 35 feet. They're hardy from Zone 4 south. All have long, sharp thorns that make excellent barrier hedges. Paul's Scarlet hawthorn is the only hawthorn that doesn't have white bloom.

LOCUST
(Gleditsia sp.)
The honey locust has been widely recommended as a substitute for American elms lost to Dutch elm disease. Ask your nurseryman for a thornless, podless variety because some are messy trees—constantly dropping twigs and seedpods.

Moraine and Sunburst are good choices; both are hardy from Zone 4 south. Honey locust should not be confused with common black locust, which is susceptible to diseases and to infestation by borer insects.

MAPLE
(Acer sp.)
This large tree family includes several that are much sought after for their beautiful fall coloring. Most maples cast a dense shade, so it will be hard to grow a good lawn under them.

Acer rubrum, Red or Swamp Maple, hardy from Zones 3 to 9, can reach a mature height of 120 feet and is strikingly beautiful in the fall when its leaves turn to red and gold.

MAGNOLIA
(Magnolia sp.)
Magnolia grandiflora is a magnificent tree, indigenous to this country.

Its big leaves are glossy; its 8-inch, white flowers are cup-shaped and fragrant. Trees bloom heavily in late May and June. Hardy Zone 7.

M. soulangeana, Saucer Magnolia, if not a true rival for *M. grandiflora,* is nonetheless a most welcome spring sight when lavender-pink bloom opens in May, before leaves unfurl. It grows to 30 feet tall; hardy Zones 4 to 9.

OAK
(Quercus sp.)
This genus includes such a huge variety of species that it would not be possible to list them all here. Grown primarily for shade, these magnificent trees are also sought for the brilliance of fall color some kinds offer. *Quercus rubra,* Red Oak,

Zones 4 to 8, has probably the most outstanding fall coloring, its leaves turning to a deep red. Its mature height may reach 70 feet.

Q. alba, White oak, Zones 3 to 8, if grown where it can spread out in its normal growth pattern, reaches a height of 100 feet. This species is extremely long lived; many trees are still living with 7-foot diameters.

OLIVE, RUSSIAN
(Elaeagnus angustifolia)
This small, decorative tree reaches a mature height of 15 to 20 feet in Zones 3 to 9. Its silvery-green-gray foliage is deciduous, and its small egg-shaped fruits are edible and highly attractive to birds.

PINE
(Pinus sp.)
Among the many pines are some that are especially sought after for landscaping on average-size city lots. Some that are recommended: *Pinus nigra,* Austrian Pine, Zones 5 to 8, which tolerates city conditions very well, can reach 80 feet but seldom does so in cities; *P. parviflora,* Japanese White pine, Zones 5 to 8, is a grafted tree that often has graceful and unusual lines—its mature height is variable; *P. sylvestris,* or Scotch pine, Zones 3 to 7, with an irregular branching habit and reddish-brown bark, is 75 feet tall at maturity.

PLUM
(Prunus sp.)
Prunus cerasifera 'Atropurpurea,' purple-leaf plum, hardy from Zones 5 to 8, is a decorative, small tree (15 feet or less at maturity). It's useful in a landscape grouping where its purple foliage contrasts with that of other decorative trees or shrubs. *P. americana,* American wild plum (Zones 5 to 8), grows as tall as 30 feet at maturity.

POPLAR
(Populus sp.)
The Populus genus includes aspens, already discussed, and a number of other useful varieties. *Populus alba,* or white poplar, is a deciduous tree

that reaches 90 feet at maturity and adapts to seaside conditions; *Populus deltoides,* or Cottonwood poplar, is hardy from Zones 1 to 8, reaches heights of 60 feet or more, but can be a nuisance because of cotton-like material that coats seeds and is blown in every direction.

REDBUD
(Cercis sp.)
Cercis canadensis, Redbud (also called Judas tree), is hardy from Zones 4 to 9. Its pea-like flowers—a combination of purple and pink—appear in April, before the tree leafs out. Its mature height is 40 feet. White- and pink-blooming varieties exist but are rather rare. Redbuds are attractive as single trees or planted in a group. *Cercis chinensis,* Chinese redbud, is less hardy, Zones 6 to 10; has bigger bloom than *C. canadensis;* but is more a shrub than a tree.

SPRUCE
(Picea sp.)
Picea abies, the Norway Spruce, is an extremely popular evergreen. It's pyramidal in form, reaching heights up to 150 feet in the forest, but considerably less in urban locations. *P. pungens,* the Colorado spruce (Zones 1 to 6), is a magnificent tree. Its widely used varieties include the Colorado Blue Spruce and Koster's Blue Spruce. Both should be planted well away from the house so the tree has plenty of space to spread its branches.

WILLOW
(Salix sp.)
Salix alba, White willow, hardy in Zones 4 to 8, has narrow leaves with whitish undersides. *S. alba 'vitellina,'* Golden willow, has yellow twigs that are colorful in winter. Each will reach 75 feet. *S. babylonica,* or Weeping willow (Zones 4 to 8), grows to 18 feet.

Shrubs

ALTHEA
(Hibiscus syriacus)
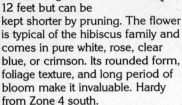
This tree-like shrub is often called Rose of Sharon. It blooms all summer and into the fall. Its mature height is 12 feet but can be kept shorter by pruning. The flower is typical of the hibiscus family and comes in pure white, rose, clear blue, or crimson. Its rounded form, foliage texture, and long period of bloom make it invaluable. Hardy from Zone 4 south.

AZALEA
(Rhododendron sp.)
These brilliantly flowered evergreen shrubs are hardy to Zone 5. A well-drained acid soil and light shade are essential for healthy growth and bloom. There are both tall and short varieties, so they can be used in any planting scheme. Choice of color is almost unlimited. The glossy foliage is attractive year round. Avoid digging near azaleas' shallow roots.

BARBERRY
(Berberis sp.)
Most varieties of this dependable shrub are hardy from Zone 4 south and evergreen from Zone 6 south. Even in hot dry zones, its leaves are attractive all summer. It's subject to very few plant diseases, and insects are no problem. Its tiny thorns make an excellent traffic barrier. Some grow to 5 or 6 feet tall, but there are dwarf varieties that can be kept to just a foot in height. Both red- and green-leaved varieties are available. All do best in full sun but grow well with just a few hours of direct sun.

BEAUTY BUSH
(Kolkwitzia amabilis)
Arching branches of this 10-foot spreading shrub are heavily laden with pink and white flowers in spring. Not choosy about soil, this vigorous shrub grows rapidly when planted in full sun. This is one of the best choices for a big screening job. It gets wide (up to 8 feet), so be sure you have plenty of space before planting. Can be trimmed to keep it in bounds.

BOXWOOD
(Buxus sp.)
Common boxwood, *Buxus sempervirens,* is a centuries-old favorite for edging formal garden beds or for hedges. This small-leaved, evergreen shrub is hardy to Zone 5. It can be pruned to any height (1 foot to 6 feet), so it lends itself to many garden situations. Korean boxwood, *B. microphylla 'koreana,'* is hardy in Zone 4. Space 3 feet apart for a hedge; a foot apart for edging.

COTONEASTER
(Cotoneaster sp.)
Many shapes and sizes make this versatile plant invaluable in the landscape. There are both tall- and low-spreading kinds. All have small flowers in spring followed by bright berries. Foliage is glossy and evergreen in mild climates. Most are hardy into Zone 4. *Cotoneaster dielsianus* reaches 4 to 6 feet in height. The rock cotoneaster, *C. horizontalis,* grows just a foot or so high and drapes beautifully over walls.

CURRANT, ALPINE
(Ribes alpinum)
Hardy from Zone 2 south, this shrub grows equally well in sun or shade. It is easy to keep in bounds because it grows slowly, so is an excellent choice for a hedge. The dark green leaves have a fine texture and contrast well with other shrubs. Its greenish-yellow flowers are attractive but not showy. Plant 2 feet apart for a dense hedge.

DAPHNE
(Daphne sp.)
Valued for its fragrant spring bloom and attractive green foliage, daphne is hardy from Zone 4 south. It's evergreen even in cold zones, if given some winter protection. A dwarf type, Ruby Glow, is only a foot tall and has white to pink, fragrant blooms. All daphnes prefer lightly shaded locations in well-drained soil but can take full sun in the more northern areas. Buy container-grown or balled-and-burlapped plants; bare-root plants are slow or impossible to get off to a good start. Water sparingly during summer months.

DEUTZIA
(Deutzia gracilis)
Handsome to use as foundation plantings or specimens, the slender Deutzia puts on a great show of dainty white flowers in the spring. Its fountain shape is attractive even when not in bloom. It seldom grows more than 3 feet tall and prefers light shade but will do well in full sun. Branches can be forced into bloom when brought inside in midwinter. Hardy in Zone 4.

FORSYTHIA
(Forsythia sp.)
Their bright yellow blossoms are harbingers of spring in most sections of the country. If untrimmed, growth can reach 8 feet. Beatrix Farrand, Lynwood Gold, and Spring Glory are among the most popular of the forsythia varieties. All are hardy in Zone 4 and bloom profusely when grown in full sun or partial shade. Forsythias are especially nice when used in a mixed-shrub border. Branches force easily in very early spring.

HONEYSUCKLE
(Lonicera sp.)
Both shrub and vine forms of honeysuckle are excellent. Flowers on the vines are more showy than those of the shrub. The red or orange fruits are attractive and provide food for birds. Tatarian honeysuckle, *Lonicera tatarica,* is one of the best hardy shrubs (Zone

3) for informal hedges. It will grow 9 feet tall or can be trimmed to half that height.

HOLLY
(Ilex sp.)
Both tree and shrub forms of holly grow well in acid soil, rich with humus. There are many varieties, each with distinctive shapes and leaves. Their lustrous foliage is handsome year round, and bright berries make the plants attractive in fall and winter. All trim beautifully to desired shapes and sizes. Most are hardy to Zone 5.

HYDRANGEA
(Hydrangea sp.)
Most are of medium size but produce quantities of large white, pink, or blue flower clusters. Hydrangeas prefer a rich, moist soil and a lightly shaded location. When top growth dies back in the winter, cut off dead branches after new growth starts in spring.

JUNIPER
(Juniperus sp.)
Junipers are the favorite evergreen plants for foundation plantings. There are ground-hugging types, low- and tall-spreading kinds, and tall slender ones that are excellent as accent plants.

All junipers are hardy into Zone 4. The creeping juniper, *Juniperus horizontalis,* is hardy in Zone 2, as are the many varieties of the common juniper, *Juniperus chinensis.*

LILAC
(Syringa sp.)
Hybrids of the common lilac, *Syringa vulgaris,* are the queens of the lilacs. So varied are color choices—from pure white to deep purple, with blue, pink, and rose in between— that making a choice is difficult. The Chinese lilac, *S. x chinensis,* has smaller blossoms but is excellent as

a shrub border; its smaller size makes it easier to manage. Lilacs prefer full sun and must have cold winters for good bloom.

MAGNOLIA, STAR
(Magnolia stellata)
This lovely plant reaches a height of about 15 feet at maturity but grows very slowly and retains a shrub form for many years. It's hardy as far north as Zone 4 and has 3-inch, fragrant white blooms in early spring before the leaves appear. The foliage is glossy and turns bronze in the fall. For best growth, good soil and drainage are essential.

MOCKORANGE
(Philadelphus sp.)
Represented by a number of types varying in size and growth habits, this beautiful spring-flowering shrub is one of the most widely grown shrubs in Zones 4 to 8. There are several sizes with double or single blossom types available.

QUINCE, FLOWERING
(Chaenomeles speciosa)
Among the first flowering shrubs to bloom in spring, quinces are widely available in a range of colors— pink, red, orange, and white. All are hardy from Zone 4 south. They need no special care but grow best in full sun. May be trimmed, used as hedges, or grown as specimen plants.

PRIVET
(Ligustrum sp.)
Privet is popularly used as a hedge because it's readily available and relatively inexpensive. This shade-tolerant, hardy shrub will grow in soil of any type. Grown primarily as a trimmed, formal hedge, it also looks great untrimmed. Privet species come as low as two feet, and the glossy privet grows to 30 feet.

SPICEBUSH
(Lindera benzoin)
Hardy from Zone 4 south, it may reach 12 feet. Has aromatic, small, yellow bloom in spring before leaves appear. Scarlet fruit follows. Leaves turn a golden yellow in fall. Tolerates partial shade but prefers sun.

SPIREA
(Spiraea sp.)
Bridal wreath spirea presents arching sprays of white flowers that cover the shrub in spring. It reaches a maximum height of 6 feet and is hardy from Zone 4 south. The Anthony Waterer spirea grows just 2 feet tall. Its 6-inch flat clusters of red blossoms appear in late spring.

VIBURNUM
(Viburnum sp.)
Viburnum sieboldi is one of the hardiest and handsomest of all viburnums. It has flat panicles of bloom in May or June. Grows to 15 feet in Zone 4. Other desirable varieties include *V. carlesi,* which has sweet-scented bloom and grows to 5 feet tall; and *V. plicatum 'tomentosum,'* offers lacy, white bloom.

WEIGELA
(Weigela sp.)
Trumpet-shaped flowers in shades of pink, rose, and red appear in spring, often followed by intermittent bloom all summer. Plant in sun in moist soil. Bristol Ruby and Boskoop Glory are among highly desirable varieties.

YEW
(Taxus sp.)
The best evergreen for shade, although it does well in morning sun in northern areas. There are both upright and spreading types to use as foundation plantings or hedges. Taxus has several dwarf or short varieties that can be used as hedges or specimen plants. *Taxus canadensis* and *T. cuspidata* are two desirable low-growing kinds.

75

Perennial Vines

BIG LEAF WINTERCREEPER
(Euonymus fortunei)
One of the hardiest of all evergreen vines, it is hardy from Zone 5 south. It holds winter foliage best if planted out of bright sunlight on the north or east sides of buildings. It can scale a 20-foot wall but is easily kept in bounds by yearly pruning. Branches cling by aerial rootlets.

BITTERSWEET
(Celastrus sp.)
The native American bittersweet is hardy in Zones 3 to 8 and does well in full sun or part sun. Buy several plants as male and female flowers occur on separate plants, and you need both to have berries.

A superior variety, *Celastrus rosthornianus,* or Chinese bittersweet, is hardy from Zone 5 south and is one of the most prolific fruiting varieties, bearing yellow and orange-scarlet berries over the entire vine, not just in small clusters.

CLEMATIS
(Clematis sp.)
Hybrids of this most colorful vine come in a wide range of colors, including white.
They're easy to grow if you supply rich, loose soil and full sun. The clematis is another plant that likes to have its foliage in the sun and its roots in the shade, so mulch the soil well. When planting, replace earth with rich loam, adding a cup of lime to the loam. Install supports before planting. After planting, top-dress with peat mixed with a little well-rotted cow manure. Water deeply each week during dry spells.

DUTCHMAN'S PIPE
(Aristolochia durior)
Also known as pipe vinegets, the common name comes from its curved, yellowish-green flowers that are up to 3 inches long. Hardy from Zone 4 south, it is a vigorous vine that grows as high as 30 feet. Its leaves are large and heart-shaped and offer dense shade for an arbor-covered patio.

GRAPE
(Vitis sp.)
In addition to grape vines grown for their edible fruits, the Japanese ornamental grape (zones 5 to 8) is a woody vine with leaves a foot across that turn a bright scarlet in autumn. Blue-black fruit is not edible.

To grow edible grape vines, consult your state extension service for advice on varieties best suited to your area. To get a good crop of fruit, top growth must be cut back severely in late February. If pruned in spring, the cut stems bleed sap for a week or more. This greatly weakens the plant. When trimming, leave just one strong cane with two buds.

HONEYSUCKLE
(Lonicera sp.)
Japanese honey- suckle is one of the hardiest vines—related to the shrubs of the same name. It is a semi-evergreen vine to 30 feet, bearing fragrant white bloom in June. It can easily become a pest because its growth is so rampant. The variety Hall's Honeysuckle is not as rampant but still must be kept in bounds by regular pruning.

Lonicera pericylmenum, commonly called woodbine, belongs to the same family. It is a woody climber to 20 feet, bearing fragrant white blooms touched with red in terminal clusters in June, red berries in fall. Hardy, Zones 5 to 8.

IVY
(Hedera helix)
Varieties of this ivy give us a number of nearly indispensable perennial vines. As for English ivy, it is hardy as far north as New York City, but north of Zone 6, it may not be dependably so. Try a few plants to see.

Two other plants, Boston ivy and Baltic ivy, are not true ivies but are so called because their foliage resembles that of ivy. Both are hardy in Zone 5. If planting Boston ivy, use it only on stock or brick surfaces. It clings by rootlike holdfasts and, if grown on a wood surface, may cause the wood to rot.

ROSES, CLIMBING
(Rosa sp.)
Climbing roses include at least 8 general classes, many of which are difficult to put into groups that do not overlap.
Ramblers grow faster than any other climbers, sometimes developing canes as long as 20 feet in a season. They're among the most hardy of climbers but are susceptible to mildew. Large-flowered climbers grow more slowly. Pillars have an upright, restrained growth that suits them for training on posts. Trailers make pleasing covers for banks and walls. Bloom is less attractive than that of some other roses, but they're easy to grow. Hybrid tea, floribunda, and polyantha climbers are mutations of bush types and have the same characteristics and needs.

TRUMPET VINE
(Campsis sp.)
Also called by the common name, trumpet creeper. It is hardy from Zones 4 to 9. A tall, woody
creeper, it seldom produces its characteristic orange-scarlet, trumpet-shape bloom until the vine is about five years old. Flowers are produced in striking clusters, with individual florets measuring up to 2 inches across. Mme. Galen, a hybrid, is as hardy but bears even more dramatic and abundant bloom of larger size. Grow these vines in sun or partial sun, trained on trellises.

VIRGINIA CREEPER
(Parthenocissus quinquefolia)
Also called American ivy or woodbine, it is hardy from Zone 4 south. It grows tall, with each leaf divided into five leaflets. It clings to walls and trees by means of disk-tipped holdfasts. Foliage turns an attractive shade of scarlet in autumn. This vine adapts well to sun or partial shade and needs little maintenance or special care other than an occasional shearing to keep the appearance neat.

Annual Vines

BALLOON VINE
(*Cardiospermum halicacabum*)
Its common name comes from the puffy, 1-inch seed balls that resemble miniature balloons. This fast-growing annual shoots to 8 or 10 feet if you plant it in rich, well-drained soil in full sun. It endures heat and drought.

BLACK-EYED SUSAN VINE
(*Thunbergia alata*)
Also called clock vine, it scatters golden yellow flowers among crisp green leaves. Orange and white varieties are also available. This fast-growing vine climbs 8 feet in a season. It tolerates poor soil but blooms most prolifically in good garden soil. It is one of the better choices for sunny spots.

CANARY-BIRD VINE
(*Tropaeolum peregrinum*)
Related to garden nasturtiums, this annual vine takes its common name from the look of its flowers—up to an inch across—with two big petals and three smaller, plus a greenish spur. It's a fine houseplant, as well as an outdoor vine that may reach 8 feet in a season. *Tropaeolum majus*, a close relative known as indian cress, comes in both dwarf and climbing forms, has big five-petaled, scarlet-yellow flowers. Needs sun.

CARDINAL CLIMBER
(*Ipomoea x multifida*)
White-throated, cardinal-red flowers over an inch across offer attractive contrast to finely cut, shiny dark green foliage. Grow it in full sun. It will need a trellis for support and may grow to 15 feet high in a single growing season. This is a vine recommended for display, rather than one that will provide any appreciable amount of shade. Plant seed outdoors when soil has warmed. Sow seed ½ inch deep.

CATHEDRAL BELLS
(*Cobea scandens*)
Also known as the cup-and-saucer vine, it is so called because of the odd shape of its blooms. Blooms 2¼ inches wide open in a shade of green that becomes purple-blue as flowers mature. Plum-shaped fruit appears later in the season. It reaches a height of 20 feet.

CYPRESS VINE
(*Ipomoea quamoclit*)
A relative of the cardinal climber, it has trumpet-shaped bloom that may measure more than an inch across and is usually sold in seed of mixed colors, including white, rose, and red. Fernlike foliage makes a nice contrasting background for flowers. Grows to 10 feet in a season. It is recommended for decorative use, rather than to provide shade.

GOURDS, ORNAMENTAL
(*Cucurbita* genus)
These decorative gourds are grown from seed sown outdoors when the soil has warmed. Grow in highly attractive way by training them on an arbor, so fruits hang in view below the foliage. Gourd seeds come in mixed varieties, including calabash, dipper, Hercule's club, and penguin. A range of interesting shapes and color qualifies them as good subjects for fall table decorations. Seed for bottle gourds and smaller gourds are also widely available.

MARBLE VINE
(*Diplocyclos palmatus*)
The small round fruits of this fast-growing vine account for the common name. It may be used to shade a porch or patio or to screen fences. Fruits are generously produced and are apple-green with white stripes. As fruits age, colors change to amber and cream. Needs full sun.

MOONFLOWER
(*Ipomoea alba*)
If you like to sit on your porch or patio during long summer evenings, you'll like the moonflower. Its huge white blooms (up to 6 inches across) open each evening, remain open till noon the next day.

MORNING GLORY
(*Ipomoea purpurea*)
Ipomea is an easy-to-grow climbing vine available in Heavenly Blue, Pearly Gates, Scarlett O'Hara, and in the Early Call series whose flowers bloom earlier than the others listed before. All like a soil that's not too rich and in full sun. They open early and close when the sun goes down.

NASTURTIUM
(*Tropaeolum majus*)
This vine is most effective grown in hanging pots or planted in raised beds and allowed to train downward. Besides the familiar yellow and orange shades, you may choose red, salmon, white, and even purple. Plant seed outdoors when soil has warmed. Plant in sun if summers are cool; in partial shade where summers are hot.

SCARLET RUNNER VINE
(*Phaseolus coccineus*)
The scarlet runner beans from which this vine is grown are close relatives of snap beans. It grows quickly to a height of 10 feet to provide shade or privacy and puts out scarlet bloom all summer. Grow as you would pole beans.

SWEET PEA
(*Lathyras odoratus*)
This old favorite is now available in improved climbing types that will bloom for lengthy periods, taking hot spells in stride. Royal Family is a recommended new hybrid. Seeds are ordinarily sold as a mix, but colors are harmonious. Plant seed as early in spring as soil can be worked, in sun or partial sun.

Ground Covers

AJUGA
(Ajuga reptans)
This most desirable ground cover is often called bugleweed or carpet bugle. It adapts to sun or shade, sends up spires of bright 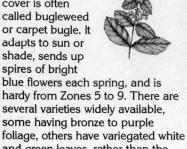 blue flowers each spring, and is hardy from Zones 5 to 9. There are several varieties widely available, some having bronze to purple foliage, others have variegated white and green leaves, rather than the green leaves of the more commonly grown ones. A spectacular way to plant these in a large area is to plant areas with two or three varieties to create a multicolored pattern.

Ajuga spreads rapidly from runners, so don't plant where its spreading habit could make it a pest.

There are also varieties that have white or pink bloom, though the blue bloom is most widely sold.

BEARBERRY
(Arctostaphylos uva-ursi)
Another common name for this plant, kinnikinick, is the name the Indians gave it. Actually a small, shrub-like plant, it is horizontal, rather than upright in growth, sending out runner stems up to 6 feet long, rooting at the joints. In spring it puts out terminal clusters of small pink or white flowers. Its evergreen foliage turns a bronzy hue in autumn.

Acid soil is essential for growth. Hardy from Zones 2 to 5.

BISHOP'S WEED
(Aegopodium podagraria)
Goutweed is another common name for it. This sturdy, attractive plant often thrives where other plants often fail. It will take morning sun but likes shade best. Underground runners spread so rapidly that it can become a pest, even in poor soil. Plant it where roots can be contained, so avoid using in a border with other plants. The white and green variegated plants grow from 8 to 10 inches tall and are hardy from Zone 4 south.

EUONYMUS, winter creeper
(Euonymus fortunei, 'colorata')
Forms a tight mat of evergreen foliage in partially shaded area; it is evergreen even in northern states. Spreads rapidly by rooting along its stems. Cuttings taken in June or July root easily in sand. Space the young plants a foot apart. There are several varieties of creeping euonymus; some grow just 4 or 5 inches tall. All prefer partial shade.

FESTUCA
(Festuca ovina)
Fescue grass is one of a number of ornamental grasses that make excellent ground covers. Narrow leaf blades form an 8-inch mound that has a definite bluish cast. It needs sun or partial sun to flourish. It makes a handsome ground cover or edging for mixed perennial borders. It grows 12 inches tall and is hardy in Zone 4.

May be grown from seed or purchased as young plants. Space plants a foot apart in spring. With closer spacing, you lose the mounded, clumpy look that's important for the appearance of this grass. A mulch of straw will help it through the winter in colder areas.

GINGER, WILD
(Asarum canadense)
A low-growing perennial with spreading habit. It has large leaves of fairly light green and grows to 6 inches in height. In April these plants bear small maroon flowers buried under the thick mat of leaves.

Wild ginger needs light shade and a moist soil rich in humus. It must have good drainage. Hardy in Zone 2. Start with divisions planted in early spring, spacing them 8 inches apart. A small clump is a beautiful addition to the foreground of the shady border. Although the blooms are hidden, the foliage and low height adds fine contrasts with adjacent plantings. It does not spread fast enough to be a problem. It makes an exceptional ground cover for problem slopes under trees.

HYPERICUM
(Hypericum sp.)
Called St. John's-Wort, this family of plants includes several ornamental shrubby or herbaceous plants that serve well as ground covers. Some are evergreen in milder climates. One variety, Golden Flower, survives winter weather as far north as Zone 5. All bear bright yellow flowers in spring. These plants tolerate sandy soil and partial shade. Start with young plants, spacing them 2 feet apart. Increase by cuttings from established plants. Root in moist sand.

IVY
(Hedera helix)
English ivy is a vining plant that also serves as an attractive ground cover. It's been widely used on our West Coast and is hardy as far north as Zone 5. Few ivies will tolerate full sun, so plant where there is protection from the midday sun. Try planting only a few starts, checking to see whether they survive the winter before you plant in large quantities. Start with small plants, spacing them 12 to 18 inches apart. Feed each spring; water when weather is hot and dry, but to reduce the danger of disease, do this in the morning so foliage will be dry by night. Feed new plantings each spring until they make a solid cover. Feed lightly thereafter to maintain the vigor of the planting.

JUNIPER
(Juniperus sp.)
The junipers include several prostrate kinds that make impressive ground covers. Creeping Juniper, *Juniperus horizontalis*, is one of the most desirable kinds in Zones 3 to 9. Sprawling in habit, it grows to about 18 inches high. One plant will eventually cover an area about 3 feet square.

There are several varieties of this species, including alpina, which grows just one foot tall, and Wakegan, which has a bluish cast but a purplish hue in winter.

J. Chinensis 'procumbens' Japgarden is hardy from Zones 4 to 9. It grows to a mature height of about 14 inches, with needles that have a bluish tone.

All junipers need some pruning each year to keep them in bounds. Feed evergreens with fertilizer formulated for them.

Until plants are well established, keep them watered in dry seasons, particularly in late fall, so they go into winter with an ample supply of moisture.

LILY-OF-THE-VALLEY
(Convallaria majalis)
Loved for its intensely fragrant spring bloom and white, bell-shaped florets on flower scapes that rise above the stiffly upright, whorled green leaves. Just 2 or 3 blooming stems make a delightful bouquet in a bud vase. When not in bloom, its foliage forms a most attractive ground cover in shaded areas of Zones 4 to 8. This dependable plant will grow rather well in the most dense shade but prefers to get some sun. Include some small patches in your perennial borders, or use as a ground cover around tree trunks.

MOSS PINK
(Phlox subulata); also called moss phlox,
This low-growing evergreen plant is covered each spring with pink or crimson bloom. Less common are blue and white varieties. It is a favorite ground cover because of its tight, low growth. It spreads horizontally, and wherever stems touch the earth, they send down roots. This means that it can be counted on to spread over a large area. Set out new plants in spring, spacing them apart. Hardy, Zones 4 to 9.

A relative, *phlox divaricata,* or sweet william, is also a ground cover for shady wild gardens. Lavender-blue bloom is common; pink and white are rare. The plant itself is ground hugging. In spring it sends up tall bloom stems.

PACHYSANDRA
(Pachysandra terminalis)
For shaded areas, pachysandra is an outstanding ground cover. Its foliage remains green all year round, and it is hardy from Zone 5 to Zone 9. Height at maturity is about 8 inches. Set rooted cuttings 6 to 12 inches apart. The larger the area covered by this handsome plant, the more effective it is. Once established, the planting needs little attention other than water during dry spells.

It is easy to propagate by taking cuttings from established plants in spring. It won't take long to cover a large area. Root cuttings in moist sand or vermiculite.

POLYGONUM
(Polygonum auberti)
Also known as silver fleece vine and lace vine, this plant is hardy from Zones 4 to 8, and if allowed to sprawl rather than climb, it serves as ground cover in an area that receives sun or partial sun.

In August, it produces clusters of greenish-white, fragrant bloom.

SEDUM
(Sedum sp.)
The sedum family is so large it's impossible to list all of them that would make attractive ground covers. They like sun and sandy, well-drained soil.

Hardy from Zones 5 to 8 are varieties known as Mossy Stonecrop and Golden Moss. They form evergreen mats of fleshy leaves capable of storing water in dry spells. Clusters of yellow flowers appear in June.

Sedum spathulifolium 'Cape Blanco,' an English import, is an extremely good-looking, low-growing variety. It forms rosettes of blue-green foliage and is covered with yellow bloom in May and June. Spreads slowly.

SILVER MOUND ARTEMESIA
(Artemesia schmidtiana 'nana')
Neat mounds of ferny foliage of a

very pale, silvery gray make this artemesia a popular choice. Each mound is about 8 inches high and 12 inches in diameter.

Plants require no more than average garden soil, good drainage, and sun. Hardy, Zones 4 to 9.

STRAWBERRY
(Fragaria sp.)
Low-growing, this small-leaf variety gets just 2 or 3 inches tall. It can be a good ground cover in a wide range of soil types and growing conditions. It spreads rapidly by runners.

In spring, yellow flowers are followed by small, red fruits on stems above the mat of foliage.

F. vesca, the wood strawberry, is also a ground cover for shade. White flowers in spring are followed by very small fruits. Hardy, Zones 5 to 8.

VINCA MINOR
(Vinca sp.)
Often called by the common name of periwinkle, this evergreen ground cover has a trailing habit and roots at every stem node. This growth habit lets you propagate by cuttings. Space newly rooted cuttings or divisions 8 to 12 inches apart. Most varieties have blue flowers in spring, but there are white-flowered varieties, also.

Vinca minor tolerates poor soil, sun, or shade. Hardy to Zone 4, with winter protection.

VIOLET
(Viola sp.)
The common violet has a number of varieties. Some bear deep purple bloom; others, bloom of varying shades of blue and lavender or white. All grow well in poor soil in shade and can be used satisfactorily as ground cover because the foliage stays attractive. A big plus for violets is that they're free! Zones 3 to 10.

How to Start Annuals

One of the best ways to stretch your garden budget is to grow annuals from seed. You can get many plants from a single packet of seed—and have a lot of fun in the process. Start some indoors, but plant as many kinds as possible in the garden.

To get seed of special varieties, order from seed catalogs. And get the order in early. Try some different kinds of plants or new varieties of some old favorites every year. There are good choices on seed racks, too.

To start annuals indoors, you'll need a sunny window and some shallow containers filled with soil. An easy method is to use individual peat pots filled with soil or peat cubes, pictured *opposite*. With these, you eliminate transplanting later. Or you can use the handy starter kits available in most supermarkets.

For early planting indoors, sow the seeds six weeks before the last expected frost in your area. Then you'll have sturdy young plants to set out at planting time. If seed is started too early, your plants will be weak and leggy by planting time.

To plant seed in flats of soil, add vermiculite or perlite to the sterile soil mix. Make rows, and space the seeds in the rows. Barely cover tiny seeds; cover large seeds with at least ⅛ inch of soil. Water gently and set the flats inside clear plastic bags. Use this method with the peat pots, too. Place in bright light but out of direct sun. The high humidity eliminates watering and encourages seeds to germinate. Remove the bag as soon as the seedlings appear.

Move the flats into brighter light as the plants increase in size. Transplant into individual pots when plants have two or more true leaves. If you have spaced the seeds some distance apart, plant directly from the flat into the garden.

Many annuals, such as marigold and zinnia, grow rapidly to blooming size when planted directly in the garden border. You gain comparatively little time by starting them early inside. Make rows in the area to be planted, and space the seeds an inch or so apart. Cover the seeds with about ¼ inch of soil and firm it lightly.

When seedlings are an inch or two tall, thin the plants to stand six inches to a foot apart, depending on their ultimate size. Plant the seedlings removed elsewhere in the garden. When seedlings are growing very close together, cut the ones to be thinned out off at ground level; this eliminates damaging the roots of the plants you want left. If you have a sunny protected spot, start most annuals for your garden there, and transplant the young plants to the garden borders.

STARTING ANNUALS

When growing annuals from seed started indoors, don't plant seeds too close together. If you're growing several kinds of seeds in one container, be sure to insert labels identifying where one variety ends and the next begins. Use waterproof ink to write the name of the plant on the stake, or wrap and secure the seed packet to stake. Also jot down the date you planted the seeds. Slide planted flat inside a clear plastic bag.

After you remove the plastic covering, keep the soil moist but not soggy. The first leaves to appear are not true leaves; the next ones are. At this time, use a spoon to lift out tiny seedlings and transplant into individual pots, being careful not to break off tender roots. Hold onto the seedling as you sift the soil about its roots. Fill peat pots to within ½ inch of the top to allow for watering. Set plants in strong light.

START SEED IN POTS

These "pots" are net-enclosed peat-moss balls that start as flat disks. To use, soak them in water until they swell to the right size. Then set on a bed of moist peat and vermiculite.

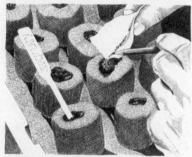

Use a folded piece of paper and a pencil as aids when planting. Tap out no more than two or three seeds into each pot. Press seed lightly into the peat moss with pencil. Many seedlings are hard to identify; use plant labels so you'll be able to tell one variety from another. Add no fertilizer.

Place the flat containing starter pots planted with seed in a sunny window or under artificial light. If in a window, turn occasionally to keep growth straight. Seedlings started in individual pots grow from seed to outside planting without transplanting, so they're usually more vigorous.

MOVING PLANTS TO GARDEN

If you used the net cubes to start your annuals, set these into garden beds intact. If the plants are in peat pots, break off the pot rim and remove the bottom before planting. This puts the roots in direct contact with the garden soil. To transplant from flats, break away one side of the container, and lift out individual plants with a fork or knife, *below*. Keep as many roots as possible on the plant. Place the freshly lifted plant into its garden bed immediately, and water soon after planting. A loose mulch over the bed or around each plant keeps the soil evenly moist during this critical stage.

PESTS AND DISEASES

Annuals are not subject to many pests or diseases. If serious trouble develops, spray the garden with a general pesticide. Repeat as needed, following the manufacturer's instructions. Pull out and destroy all plants that are badly infested with insects or infected by disease. Control mealy bugs and red spider mites by directing a sharp spray of water at the plants. Remove cutworms and caterpillars one at a time, and destroy them.

Slugs and snails are difficult to control, but you can keep their numbers down by spreading poison bait under their favorite plants. These pests like to spend the day in a moist, shady spot, so set traps for them by placing eight-inch-square boards around the garden. Just lift the boards occasionally and kill them.

GET BUSHY GROWTH

To get bushy, sturdy plants, pinch the growing tip from young bedding plants when they are six to eight inches tall. Pinching encourages the plant to send out side shoots along the stem. This increases the number of growing tips and the blooming potential of the plant. With some plants, such as impatiens and wax begonias, take a cutting from the top of the plant when you pinch it. The cutting should be at least two inches long. Root cuttings in vermiculite.

Some plants, such as marigolds, branch out naturally, and so don't need pinching. Never pinch tomatoes; they will just send out more suckers. Pinch leggy plants anytime.

SUMMER CARE

Pinch or cut off all faded flowers so the plant will produce more bloom and fewer seeds. In midsummer—when flower production slows—renew the plants by feeding them and cutting back all leggy stems. (Trimming helps petunias in particular.) Water thoroughly. Do not overfeed annuals. Many will put out abundant growth, but few flowers, if they get too much nitrogen.

A summer mulch will mean less watering for annual plantings, but you must still keep a close eye on soil moisture. Water deeply when it's necessary, but allow the ground to become a little dry between waterings. This encourages the annuals to send their roots deep into the soil.

Perennial Care

It's difficult to generalize about caring for perennials because each plant is different. However, these are some common guidelines you should follow.

First, set plants at the proper depth—at the level they had been growing if you are transplanting or buying plants from a local nursery. Always check reference books for the correct depths.

Next provide for root growth. Dig a hole several inches wider and deeper than the spread of the roots, and enrich the soil for the planting hole with compost or peat moss. Fan roots out so they can grow in all directions. It often helps to firm a low cone of soil at the bottom of the hole; this keeps the crown of the plant from settling and helps you place roots more easily. Then gradually fill in with soil.

Avoid shocking the plant. Don't let roots dry or break off. They're the lifeline to food, moisture, and good health.

Choose a cool or cloudy day for planting. If it's warm and sunny, keep roots covered with water-soaked newspapers until you're ready to plant. Lift plants gently and set at the level they had been growing.

Gradually cover the roots with soil, and gently firm it into place. Water thoroughly after transplanting, and continue to water daily until plants are established. If soil settles, keep adding more until the ground is level with the bed.

If you plant in fall, use stakes to mark the location of each new plant. Some emerge quite late in the spring, and you can easily forget where they were placed. Keep newly set plants watered until there has been a hard freeze. Cover them with a light mulch for the winter, then remove it in the spring as green shoots appear. But keep some mulch handy to re-cover young, tender shoots in case of late frost.

Don't use raked leaves as mulch. Winter snows and rains can pack them into a tight, soggy mass that can smother many plants. Much better materials to use for winter mulch are straw, hay, pruned branches of evergreens, or bark chips. The purpose of a winter mulch is to maintain an even soil temperature. Alternate freezing and thawing can lift plants out of the ground.

HOW TO DIVIDE PEONIES IN THE FALL

Peonies left undisturbed over long periods of time often bloom well. But it's good practice to lift and divide herbaceous peonies once every five or six years during the fall only. New divisions give you fresh, vigorous growth, plus more flowers.

First, dig a shallow trench just outside the edge of the clump. When the plant is completely encircled, pry under the root mass with a spade, as you lift from above, using the stems as a "handle" to pull with.

Use a hose to wash away all soil so you can clearly see where "eyes" are located on the roots. Use a sturdy, well-sharpened knife to make the divisions. To get bloom the next season, no division should have fewer than three eyes; five to eight is even better. Remember this when buying new peony plants from a nurseryman. Differences in price usually depend on the variety of plant and the number of eyes.

New introductions will also be more expensive than old favorites. Pick both early and late bloomers for a long period of peony color in the spring. If you have space, include as many different colors as you can. Choose a sunny spot for your peonies. A half day of sun is adequate; but the more sun, the better. To plant a new division, begin by digging a deep hole (two feet) and replacing the subsoil with fresh topsoil. Adding humus and bone meal to soil replaced at the bottom of the hole helps growth. Do not use peat moss or cow manure, however.

Set divisions three feet apart. Make certain that eyes are one to two inches below soil surface. Measure to be sure. Spread roots over the firm mound at the bottom of hole. Add more topsoil, and water.

Fertilize after each blooming period. In cold climates, mulch with two to four inches of straw or hay to prepare for winter.

SPACING

The space you leave between perennials varies with their spread at maturity. But all will be healthier with a little "breathing space" between themselves and their neighbors. Circulation of air greatly reduces the risks of mold and mildew. Also, proper spacing eliminates excessive competition for soil, moisture, and nutrients, so your plants can grow to specimen sizes. For help in deciding how *much* space they need, check the section entitled "ABCs."

Another topic to consider is grouping. You will always get a more attractive appearance when you group at least three plants of one kind together. And in a perennial border, you will enhance the overall effect by repeating a group of the same plants at intervals in the border (see pages 28 and 29 for perennial border plans).

WATERING

Water newly divided perennial plants *immediately* after replanting. Keep soil moist for the first month.

For beds of perennials, use a soaker hose to water plants, instead of spraying them from above. Be sure to leave the soaker hose in place long enough so water soaks the soil to a depth of several inches.

The best time to water is early morning, so water that gets onto foliage will dry before dark. Foliage should be dry before sundown.

DIVIDING

You can divide some perennials by cutting or gently pulling off sections of the crown. Use a hand fork or a sharp knife for tuberous or woody roots. Don't make too many divisions from one plant, and be sure each has enough roots to sustain fresh growth.

When dividing a perennial, wash soil away from the roots so you can see what you're doing. Direct a stream of water away from the base of the stems to avoid injuring the buds. Keep as many roots attached to each division as possible, but trim away any damaged roots. If any part looks dead or diseased, trim all the way back to clean, white tissue. Replant as soon as possible after dividing. Water regularly the first year.

SPRING DUTIES

During the first warm days of spring, start removing the winter mulch a little at a time. Remove all mulch from spring-flowering bulbs, but leave some on perennials until you are certain the really cold weather is over. This is the ideal time to feed perennials. Choose a plant food formulated for flowers, one that is high in nitrogen (over 15 percent) and releases its nutrients slowly over several months. A second feeding in early July will keep plants growing and blooming vigorously until the first frost.

Broadcast plant food between the plants at the rate recommended on the label. Work it lightly into the surface of the soil, and water in well. All perennials will benefit from these feedings, as will the annuals planted among them.

To encourage early, vigorous growth, allow the ground to be free of all mulch from mid- to late spring, so it will warm up rapidly. Wait until early summer to put on mulch that will keep borders moist and weed-free during the hot summer months.

FALL CHORES

After the first killing frost—usually preceded by several light frosts that nip the tops of plants but do not kill foliage back to the ground—it's time to "put the perennial border to bed" for the winter. First cut and remove dead stalks, cutting stems down to within four inches of the ground.

Dig all your tender bulbs and put into winter storage.

When the beds have been cleared of dead foliage and weeds, apply winter mulch.

In addition to the general mulch, there are other ways to cut down on winter losses. Several of them are described in the column at right, with accompanying illustrations. None takes much time or equipment, but each may save you the loss of a valued plant.

If fall rains have been light, deeply water your flower borders and lawn. All plants need moisture to get them through the winter.

In addition to the devices described and pictured here, use an inverted bushel basket, weighted down with a brick, to cover a tender plant.

WINTER COVER

Put a protective covering over tufts of fall growth. An inverted flowerpot over a madonna lily protects the shoot from heavy snow and mulch.

For perennial beds exposed to wind, lay sections of poultry wire over the general mulch, and weigh down at intervals with bricks or stones.

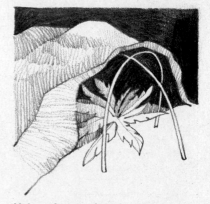

Make a frame of crossed wire loops to protect fall growth of Oriental poppies. Cover with burlap and pile soil on the edges to hold in place. Do not substitute plastic; it captures and holds heat from the sun.

83

Get Trees and Shrubs Off to a Good Start

Whether planting a big tree for shade or an ornamental tree for flowers, rapid, sturdy growth is the main concern. Extra care at planting time gets trees off to a fast start, so you can enjoy them sooner. Shrubs need early care, too.

USE THE RIGHT TREE

Success is guaranteed if the right tree is chosen for a specific spot in the landscape. If you want shade, or a tree to frame the house, choose a tall, arching tree such as an ash or hybrid locust. A cone-shaped tree (a pin oak, for instance) is fine as an accent to one side or to the rear of the garden, but its low-hanging branches make it a bad choice for the front of the house. So choose trees carefully. See the "ABCs" section on trees for help.

With shrubs, also, learn the mature heights and spreads of your choices, and plant them where there is space. Most shrubs can be kept in bounds with annual pruning, but a lot of trimming time can be eliminated if shrubs are chosen that grow to the sizes you want.

WHERE TO PLANT

Planning before planting eliminates trouble later on. Planting trees too close to a house or sidewalk results in

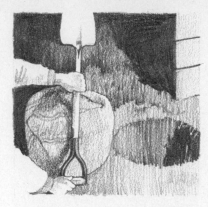

damage to shingles or gutters. Big roots can damage foundations and sidewalks. Poorly placed shrubs or evergreen trees can spread out to cover sidewalks or hide the house.

Shade trees must be planted at least 15 feet from any structure. At this distance, branches and roots pose no problems. Small ornamental trees, such as redbud and dogwood, can be planted eight feet from a house. Some trimming will be needed at this distance.

Stake your trees at planting time. The smaller the tree, the more important this is. Leave a shallow, two-foot-diameter depression around the trunk to make watering easier. Cover the soil with a three-inch-deep mulch of bark. This will also protect the tender trunk from your lawn mower.

Shrubs for foundation plantings should be set well away from the house. Center planting holes three feet from the foundation, and space large plants at least three feet apart. Measure the size of the soil ball or the plant container, *left*, and dig a planting hole a foot or so wider and a few inches deeper.

To encourage sturdy new growth, feed young trees and shrubs every year. Use a food blended for them, and follow the directions on the label. Do not overfeed. Top growth on trees can get too heavy for the trunk even if the tree is staked. Two feet of new growth each year is good enough. Some kinds will not grow this fast.

Hard dry winds and glaring sun dry out tender new foliage or the needles of newly transplanted evergreens, especially if they are being planted in late spring. Protect new growth with an anti-desiccant spray that reduces water loss through leaves and needles. This spray also reduces winter damage to evergreens. If your evergreens have some brown needles every spring, spray the foliage in late fall to eliminate the problem.

PLANTING TIPS FOR TREES AND SHRUBS

Eliminate any unnecessary cleanup when planting trees and shrubs by spreading a tarp or square of poly-ethylene-next to the planting site. Pile soil removed from the planting hole on the tarp. Grass can be damaged by soil piled on it. Put topsoil and subsoil in separate piles. Use the top-soil around the roots, and discard the subsoil by carrying it away on the tarp. Blend compost or a mix of ver-miculite and peat moss with the soil.

To set larger plants at the proper depth, use your spade handle to gauge how deep they should go. After setting the plant in the hole, lay the handle across the hole, and add or take away soil from beneath the roots to adjust the planting level.

Potted and balled-and-burlapped plants can be set with the top of the soil ball an inch or so lower than ground level. Set bare-root plants four inches lower than top roots.

To keep the soil ball intact when planting, the roots should stay wrapped or in a container until plant-ing takes place. But even with care, the roots can be damaged when they're lifted in and out of the plant-ing hole. When the hole is ready, lift or cut the plant from its container and set it in the hole. If the soil ball is wrapped in burlap, set it in the hole, and then cut the burlap away or unpin and pull it free of the trunk.

HOW TO PLANT A HEDGE

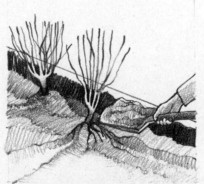

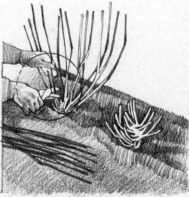

An informal hedge needs less care and requires fewer plants than a for-mal one, so it's the least expensive privacy for your backyard.

Dig planting holes for an informal hedge in staggered rows, as illus-trated, *above*. For large shrubs, plant them three to four feet apart. Eventu-ally, you'll have to prune them so they'll stay at the width you want. For year-round privacy, choose ever-greens. Plant junipers in sun; yew or hemlock, in shade.

For a formal, trimmed hedge (privet, boxwood, and upright yews are favor-ites), plants must be set so close to-gether that the best way to plant them is to dig a narrow trench. To get a tight hedge, set plants ten to 12 inches apart. Trim branches back to half their lengths after planting; this will encourage thick growth at the base. In later years, trim the base wider than the top, so light can reach the lower branches. A light feeding each spring will maintain a hedge's vigor.

Most shrubs for hedges are sold bare root—even the larger types. After planting, all branches must be cut back about half to balance the tops with roots. Otherwise, new top growth would be small, weak, and subject to drying out. As a result, the plant may die. Plant bare-root shrubs as early in the spring as possible, so new growth is established before hot weather sets in. Keep the soil evenly moist so roots have a constant sup-ply of moisture. A mulch helps, too.

85

Planting Bulbs

Tulips, hyacinths, and other spring-flowering bulbs must all be planted in the fall. Correct depth of planting is related to the size of the bulb, as the chart on the opposite page shows.

SOIL PREPARATION

Dig soil for all bulbs to full spade depth. If soil is heavy, turn under a thick layer of compost, sphagnum peat moss, or vermiculite to improve tilth. Add sand for drainage. For bulb beds, spade in a low-nitrogen fertilizer high in phosphorus and potash at the same time. Level and rake smooth.

Proper tillage can go a long way toward improving the structure of your soil. On the other hand, improper tillage can do your soil great harm.

Never till your soil when it's wet. If you squeeze a handful of soil together and it forms a sticky, compact mass, it's too wet to be worked. Heavy clay soils that are tilled when they're too wet become hard and lumpy.

But even when moisture content is right, it's possible to overwork your soil. Avoid working it so finely that it crusts after a rain. Instead, try to break up clods and level the surface without destroying the structure of the soil.

PLANTING THE TENDER BULBS

Such tender bulbs as caladiums and tuberous begonias should be started indoors six to eight weeks before the last expected frost. To mix a starting medium, use equal amounts of peat and vermiculite, adding a tablespoon of low-nitrogen fertilizer to each five pounds of the mix.

Space tubers or bulbs about five inches apart in flats. Cover with a half-inch of starting medium. Keep moist, not soggy, placing the flat in strong light, but not direct sun.

When three or four leaves have formed, carefully transplant tubers to four- or five-inch pots.

Starting tender bulbs in flats.

Transplanting from flat to pot.

PLANTING TIPS

When planting several kinds of bulbs in a bed, outline in the soil the area for each group.

Space tulips and other big bulbs fairly close (five or six inches) to get a pattern of splashy colors (wide spacing weakens their impact). Set bulbs inside outlines before planting. Plunge a garden trowel to its full depth, as shown at left; pull toward you to open a pocket and set the bulb firmly in place. Use the planting chart, *opposite,* to plant hardy bulbs at proper depths. Cover with soil. Label each grouping, or record its location on your garden plan.

Mice and chipmunks can be troublesome if you plant bulbs in quantities. The only sure way to protect newly planted bulbs from this kind of damage is to place them in baskets fashioned from hardware cloth, their tops left open. Unfortunately, this is time-consuming and expensive in large plantings.

The best bulbs for "naturalizing" are narcissus. Plant them on slopes, in grass, or under trees to give the effect of natural growth. But don't do it unless you can wait to mow the grass until the bulb foliage has yellowed, because next year's bloom depends on food produced by this year's foliage. If undisturbed, each bulb eventually forms a clump.

REPLANTING

Although digging up tulips after blooming is not recommended, it can be done. However, allow the bulb to stay in place until the foliage yellows. It's prior to the yellowing stage that a bulb builds up strength through its foliage to form bloom for the following season. Mark the variety, and lift later to replant in a permanent spot.

MAINTENANCE

In addition to applying fertilizer when you first plant tulips, feed them immediately after each bloom period ends. Water beds liberally during dry spells. A two-inch layer of mulch, such as cocoa bean hulls, straw, or ground corncobs will conserve soil moisture and will also keep down weeds. A loose mulch will also prevent mud from splashing up on the flowers.

Even with fine bulbs and the best of care, hybrid tulips tend to produce smaller blooms after a few years. When this happens, either dig and replant to space the bulbs farther apart, or discard and plant new bulbs. The old bulbs could be planted in a cutting garden, so blooms for bouquets wouldn't have to be cut from the display beds; a corner of the vegetable garden would do.

If tulips must be dug before the foliage ripens, dig a shallow trench and heel in bulbs with their foliage attached.

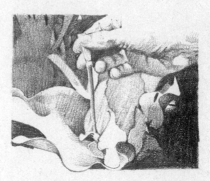

Always snap off seed heads when blooms fade. The plants' energy will then go into the bulbs and not into the production of seed.

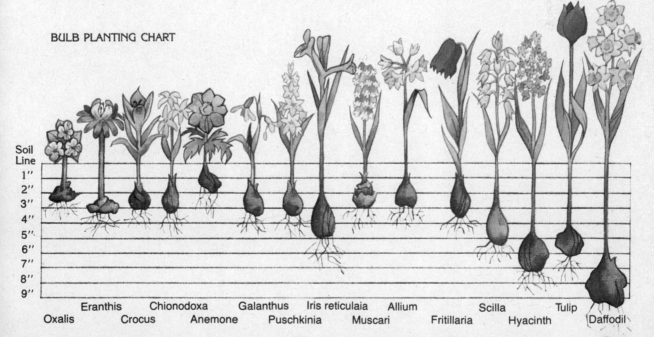

BULB PLANTING CHART

Soil Line
1"
2"
3"
4"
5"
6"
7"
8"
9"

Oxalis · Eranthis · Crocus · Chionodoxa · Anemone · Galanthus · Puschkinia · Iris reticulaia · Muscari · Allium · Fritillaria · Scilla · Hyacinth · Tulip · Daffodil

Vines and Ground Covers

Before choosing specific vines for your garden, decide how you wish to use them. Then choose the type of vine and support to fit the situation. Here are a few examples of ways to support vines with simple devices or improvisations.

MAKING A TRELLIS

There are a number of ways to make a trellis or support for vines to grow on. Chicken wire, pictured at *left, below* is one inexpensive way. Clinging vines attached to wooden walls will harm the wood. You can prevent this by putting up a chicken wire support to keep the vine away from the wall. Thread a rod through the wire, and support it from hooks in eaves or rafters. Secure the bottom of the wire support by hooks screwed into stakes driven into the ground.

Chain-link aluminum, pictured *below,* makes a very durable trellis that will be quickly covered by vines with tendrils. Clematis is one example. Attach wire to stakes at ground level, and start a new vine on it. The vine will continue to climb on its own. Many vines, particularly the annuals, grow quickly, so train them horizontally first, then vertically.

A simple wood trellis, like the one pictured directly *below,* makes a good support for twining vines. The one shown can be made of straight bamboo sticks fastened with plant ties of plastic- or paper-covered wire. When complete, set the base of this trellis directly into the ground and tie to sturdy stakes.

CLINGING AND TWINING VINES

When space permits, some vines are suitable as ground covers. Ivy and euonymus can be used this way.

Some vines respond to tight trimming, and can be treated as espaliers. Plant with the finished design in mind, and start the first growth of each plant aimed in the right direction. Regular pruning of wandering shoots is necessary to maintain the established design.

Vines that cling by adhesive disks (Boston ivy, silver vein creeper, Virginia creeper) and those with rootlike holdfasts (euonymus, Baltic ivy, climbing hydrangea) should be grown on masonry walls only. If your home is made of wood, use only vines that can be supported on trellises. Hinge the trellis at the bottom, so it can be detached and laid down during painting or repair work.

Encourage growth of new vines by feeding them generously the first few years. Feed mature vines lightly each spring to maintain their vigor.

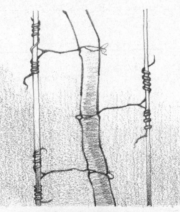

Clinging tendrils
Bittersweet
Clematis
Grape
Passion-vine

Twining
Actidinia
Honeysuckle
Silver-lace vine
Wisteria

TRAINING VINES TO CLIMB MASONRY WALLS

Before planting perennial vines supported by rootlike holdfasts or adhesive disks, dig the soil deeply. Add some organic matter (rich loam, peat, well-rotted manure) to loosen the soil and make it more fertile. If the vine is to climb a brick or stone wall, set the new plants close to the wall—no more than ten to 12 inches away.

Water newly set vines thoroughly, and apply plant food lightly when new growth appears. Be prepared to water frequently if overhanging eaves prevent the vine from receiving enough rainfall. Use either a soaker hose or a root feeder. Trim vines only enough to keep them in bounds. Cut out dead stems in late spring after new growth starts, so you can clearly see what is actually dead.

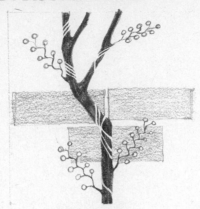

Adhesive disks
Boston ivy
Cross-vine
Silver vein creeper
Virginia creeper

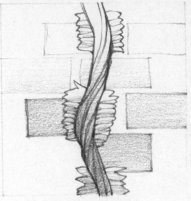

Rootlike holdfasts
Climbing hydrangea
Euonymus
Trumpet-creeper
Baltic ivy

MULTIPLY GROUND COVER

Many plants that make good ground covers send out plantlets. To get these to root quickly (increasing your supply), use small stones to hold the plantlets in place. The weight keeps the plantlet in close contact with moist soil and helps place the new plants where you want them. The sketch, *right*, illustrates how this works. The same method can be employed with ground myrtle, hay-scented fern, arenaria, and periwinkle.

PLANTING GROUND COVERS

Choose plants suited to the location. Next, prepare the soil where new plants are to be set in place by deep spading, adding leaf mold, peat, and general plant food to the soil.

Most ground covers are sold in clumps. They should be set into the ground at the level they had been growing. Water thoroughly.

Clumps may be spaced from ten to 18 inches apart, depending on how long you are willing to wait until new growth has completely covered the ground. A decorative mulch between the plants will make the area attractive until growth covers it.

Soil Care

To grow healthy, vigorous plants—from annuals to big shade trees—you need an organically enriched soil containing all the elements essential to plant growth. To find out if your soil is good, have it analyzed. In most states, the county or state extension service will do this for free or for a small fee. Take samples from several different parts of your lot and send them in, in separate containers. After the test, you should know what you'll need to add to the soil.

SOIL AMENDMENTS

You may need more than plant food to amend your soil. If it's too sandy or too high in clay content, organic matter, decomposed leaves, straw, sawdust, peat, and even sludge may also be necessary.

Animal manures are good fertilizers because they contain humus; dried manure is safer to use than fresh manure, which may burn tender plant roots. Bone meal is a good additive for plants that prefer a slightly alkaline soil. It also contains some nitrogen and phosphoric acid but no potash. Cotton-seed meal helps acid-loving plants. Lime modifies both the physical and chemical properties of the soil. It pulls together small particles of clay, thus making soil more porous.

Use perlite or vermiculite to lighten soil and keep particles apart. Urea formaldehyde is a synthetic organic fertilizer, containing a high amount of nitrogen. Because it has a built-in release control, the nitrogen is available to plants over a long period, nearly eliminating danger of burning plant tissues. It is a major nitrogen source in fertilizers. Other good additives are wood and coal ashes.

The hyphenated numbers on a bag of fertilizer indicate the pounds of nitrogen, phosphorus, and potash per hundred pounds of fertilizer—in that order. Nitrogen is necessary for the formation of new cells in all plant parts and stimulates the growth of stems and leaves. It is the nutrient most often in need of replacing.

Phosphorus strengthens both stems and roots. It also stimulates food storage and increases seed and fruit production. Next to nitrogen, phosphoric acid is the most valuable of the fertilizer constituents.

Potash, the third major element in fertilizer compounds, is needed for normal plant growth to protect the plant from disease. It also aids and stimulates the growth of sturdy roots and is essential for good flower color. Potash is a soluble mineral found in several compounds, including potassium carbonate and potassium hydroxide.

The best time to apply commercial fertilizers is several days before you put seeds or plants into the ground. Early application gives the nutrients a chance to settle into the soil and distribute themselves evenly before seed or plant roots come in contact with them. Intermediate applications may be needed for annuals and flowering perennials. Apply them as top-dressing. Keep the fertilizer six inches from the base of plants to avoid possible burning. Organic fertilizers, such as cow manure and sludge, can be used with less caution, because the nitrogen is released slowly. You can't have outstanding plants without supplemental feeding.

THE VALUES OF MULCH

The importance of a summer mulch cannot be overemphasized. A mulch all but eliminates weeds, retains soil moisture, and insulates the soil from hot sun (see drawing below). Also, the uniform texture of mulch makes your garden more attractive.

As you can see from the table, *opposite*, mulches can be made of a wide variety of materials. Some are chosen partly for good looks—cocoa bean shells, pine needles, wood or bark chips. Others are especially suited to protect against winter damage: hay, straw, pine needles. Still others work as soil conditioners: grass clippings, sawdust, peat moss, tobacco stems.

Your choices of mulching materials may depend on where you live, and the type of mulch needed, utility or decorative. Tobacco stems and pine needles are readily available in the South, while corncobs and wheat straw are common in the Midwest.

Study the chart and decide which mulch to use in the various parts of your garden to gain its benefits.

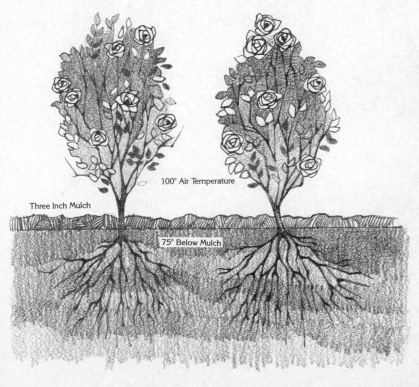

100° Air Temperature

Three Inch Mulch

75° Below Mulch

MULCH CHART

Material	Source	Recommended Depth	Characteristics
Cocoa bean shells	Candy manufacturers or garden supply centers	3 to 4 inches	Light in weight, pleasing in appearance, and of good fertilizing value. Initial chocolate odor fades after 2 weeks. May be mixed with sawdust (2 parts shells to 1 part sawdust) to prevent caking.
Corncobs (ground)	Corn-growing areas	4 to 6 inches	Coarse material with good moisture retention qualities. Can harbor injurious insect pests. Somewhat slow to break down.
Grass clippings	Lawn	2 to 3 inches	Allow to stand 2 or 3 days before using to avoid burning plants with decomposition heat. May be mixed with coarse material to reduce matting.
Hay	Farmers, cut fields, garden supply centers	6 to 8 inches	Leguminous grasses (alfalfa, clover) decay faster and supply nitrogen. Salt hay is useful because seeds will not sprout in garden soil.
Leaves	Deciduous trees	6 to 8 inches	Tends to become matted and soggy if not allowed to compost before applying. May be used immediately when mixed with another material, such as grass clippings. Oak leaves are best for acid-loving plants.
Manure (mixed with straw)	Dairy farms or stables	4 to 6 inches	Should be partially composted before applying to prevent burning plants. Good nutrient source.
Peanut shells	Peanut-growing areas, especially the South	2 to 4 inches	Easy to apply, but may have to be mixed with heavier material or weighted down with a layer of coarse mulch.
Peat moss	Garden supply centers	3 to 5 inches	Good soil conditioner, but lacking in nutrients. May dry out and repel water. Keep moist or mix with another material to avoid crusting.
Pine needles	Coniferous trees	2 inches	Excellent for strawberries and wildflowers. Will not be displaced by the wind. Decidedly acid. Allows free passage of rainfall and does not absorb moisture from the soil.
Plastic film (black)	Hardware stores and garden supply centers		Especially useful for large areas. Excellent for preserving moisture. Will warm soil (as opposed to organic materials that slow warming). Will last 4 or 5 years if properly anchored. Punch holes at low points to allow water penetration.
Sawdust	Sawmills and lumberyards	1 to 2 inches	Excellent general mulch and soil conditioner. Apply nitrogen fertilizer at regular intervals to prevent depletion of soil nitrogen.
Straw	Farms, feed stores, and garden supply centers	4 to 6 inches	Coarser than hay and longer lasting. Practical for large areas, such as the corn or pumpkin patch.
Tobacco stems	Tobacco farms	6 to 8 inches	Fairly high in nitrogen and potassium. A coarse material. Can repel insects.
Wood chips	Local utility operation, home shredder, or street department	3 to 4 inches	Much coarser than sawdust and less likely to cause nitrogen deficiency.

Soil Care, Compost

Veteran gardeners refer to compost as "gardeners' gold." This organic product of the compost heap is one of the best soil conditioners and sources of plant nutrients—a cure for many soil problems. Whether a soil is too sandy or too tight, organic matter can make it better. And what better source for this miracle additive than a compost heap? Compost is all but free because it is basically the decomposed waste material that you have gathered from your own garden.

The composting process is actually an accelerated version of what goes on in nature. Leaves, dead grass, kitchen waste, and other organic materials are attacked by billions of microorganisms during the composting process, and with the proper amounts of heat, air, water, and nitrogen, nature's wastes are gradually reduced to a form that can be used by plants. In short, nothing really ever dies: it's simply recycled.

LOCATING THE COMPOST PILE

A shady spot in an out-of-the-way corner of the garden is an ideal spot for a compost bin. In a secluded location you don't have to worry about tidiness, and the shade will help keep the pile moist. Try to locate near a water supply, so new garden refuse can be moistened as it's added. And avoid piling material against your house, garage, or fence: compost harbors wood-rotting fungi.

MAKING THE BIN

You'll hasten the decaying process and make the finished product much easier to handle if you construct a bin. All that's needed is a three- or four-sided container to keep the compost neatly in place. A three- or four-foot-square bin three feet tall will supply most gardeners with the compost they need. You can use wire fencing, wood, or concrete blocks to form the sides. One side can be left open to make working the pile easier.

Many gardeners prefer to make two bins, so compost can be easily aerated by forking it from one bin to the other, or to have one for the old usable compost and the other for the new compost.

Shown on this page are small bins contained in ornamental fencing, a permanent bin made of concrete blocks held in place by pipe stakes at the corners, and large wire bins showing construction details for the slatted board fronts. Commercially made compost bins are available.

LAYERING THE COMPOST

Organic materials for the compost are added in layers. Lawn clippings, leaves, and garden waste are the biggest sources. Each layer consists of ten or 12 inches of organic matter topped with a handful each of nitrogen fertilizer and lime. Horse and cow manure are excellent sources of nitrogen and organic matter, so add as much of each as you can find. An inch or so of garden soil placed over the pile helps to get it working.

Keep sandwiching these layers until the bin is full. Soak the compost with water as each layer is completed. And if rains are light, water each week to keep the pile thoroughly moistened.

To use your compost, simply add quantities to the soil around new plantings, dig it in around your perennials, and add to potting mixtures.

SOIL AMENDMENT CHART

Material	Amount Per 100 Sq. Ft.	When to Apply	Benefits	Remarks
ORGANIC AMENDMENTS				
Cow, sheep, horse, or hog manure	3 to 5 bushels	Two weeks before planting	Good source of nitrogen; conditions soil	Never apply fresh; should be leached by three or four rains and dried before use; add fresh to compost pile
Poultry (chicken, goose, duck, or turkey) manure	1 to 2 bushels	Two weeks before planting	Very high in nitrogen	Avoid over-application because excess amounts can "burn" roots
Compost	2 to 4 bushels	Two weeks before planting and as side-dressing	Provides major and minor nutrients; excellent soil conditioner; use as a winter mulch	Screen thoroughly to remove clumps and other unrotted material
Peat moss	20 cubic feet	When preparing soil in spring	Contains no nutrients but is excellent soil conditioner	Work thoroughly into upper 6 inches of soil
Blood meal	10 ounces	One week before planting and as side-dressing; excellent food for container-grown plants	High in nitrogen (15%)	Also useful for discouraging small animal pests, such as rabbits
Fish scraps	1¼ pounds	One week before planting and as side-dressing	High in all major nutrients: nitrogen (8%), phosphorus (13%), potassium (4%)	Bury deep in compost or garden soil to eliminate odor and to discourage animals digging for the scraps.
Cottonseed meal	5 pounds	One week before planting	High in nitrogen (8%) and phosphorus (2.5%)	Best for acid-loving plants
Bone meal	2½ pounds	Before or at planting time	High in phosphorus (24%); moderate in nitrogen (4%)	Steamed bone meal recommended; bone meal also helps reduce soil acidity
Wood ashes	4 pounds	Before or at planting time	High in potash (8%), with moderate amount of phosphorus	If allowed to stand, rain will leach out nutrients; work into soil immediately
Winter rye or vetch	Broadcast ¼ pound of seed over harrowed or raked soil	In fall after harvest and after all debris has been removed (early spring in southern regions)	Protects topsoil from erosion; provides nutrients when plowed under in spring; helps soil structure	Allow to grow to a height of 4 to 6 inches before turning under
CHEMICAL AMENDMENTS				
Lime	5 pounds or as indicated by pH soil reaction test	Before soil is turned in spring; greater amounts should be divided into two applications	Indirectly improves soil structure; increases availability of soil nutrients	Avoid over-application
Balanced fertilizer (5-10-10 or 5-10-5)	With manure, 3 to 4 pounds; without manure, 4 to 5 pounds	Rake thoroughly into top 4 inches of soil at planting or use as side-dressing	Provides nitrogen, phosphorus, and potassium for immediate use by plants	Contains few, if any, of the micronutrients; keep from direct contact with plant
Nitrate of soda	2 pounds per 100 feet of row	As side-dressing when plants are 4 inches high and every 2 weeks thereafter	Offers immediately available dose of nitrogen; especially recommended for leaf crops	Keep granules from coming into contact with leaves and roots
Ammonium sulfate	2 pounds per 100 feet of row	As side-dressing	Quick source of nitrogen; good for acid-loving plants	
Ammonium nitrate	1 pound per 100 feet of row	As side-dressing		
Phosphate rock (ground)	5 pounds per 100 feet of row	As side-dressing	A slow-release source of phosphorus	

Zone Map

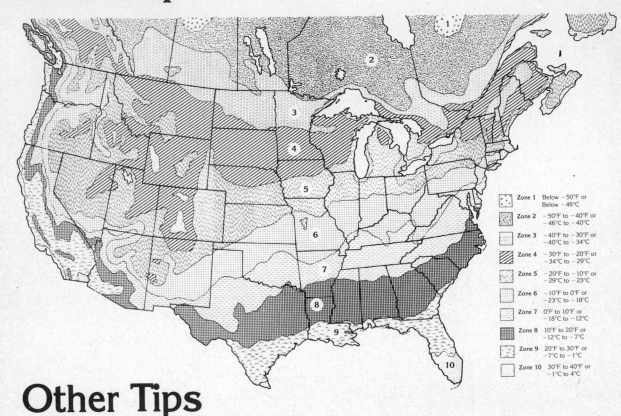

	Zone 1	Below −50°F or Below −46°C
	Zone 2	−50°F to −40°F or −46°C to −40°C
	Zone 3	−40°F to −30°F or −40°C to −34°C
	Zone 4	−30°F to −20°F or −34°C to −29°C
	Zone 5	−20°F to −10°F or −29°C to −23°C
	Zone 6	−10°F to 0°F or −23°C to −18°C
	Zone 7	0°F to 10°F or −18°C to −12°C
	Zone 8	10°F to 20°F or −12°C to −7°C
	Zone 9	20°F to 30°F or −7°C to −1°C
	Zone 10	30°F to 40°F or −1°C to 4°C

Other Tips

Throughout this book, we have referred to zone numbers representing the northern limits of the successful culture for certain plants.

Zone boundary lines are not absolute. You can expect temperatures to vary as much as 5° Fahrenheit from those given to the right of the map. You must also consider local conditions. Hills and valleys in certain areas do not always have the same high and low temperatures as those recorded at weather bureau stations.

Still other conditions to consider before selecting plants are rainfall, humidity, snow coverage, wind, and soil type. A specific perennial may survive in Zone 3 in Maine, for example, but be completely unadapted to that same zone in North Dakota—simply because of differences in rainfall and humidity.

To ensure success, start with local favorites. Your added care will help the natives prosper in domestic situations. And often they'll do better than plants brought in from distant places at surviving freakish weather, drought, flood, or early and late frosts.

Be flexible. When certain plants prosper unexpectedly in your garden, consider adding more of them—perhaps different varieties or different colors. If others do poorly, replace them with more hardy plants.

When ordering perennial plants from nursery catalogs, buy from nurseries in your general area or from those to the north of you. Plants offered in these catalogs will be hardy in your area. An exception to this would be ordering from a nursery too far to the north. Some plants, such as the lilac and peony, need winter cold to survive, so gardeners in the deep South should limit their orders to a zone or two north of them.

If you live in a borderline area and have a plant that may or may not survive the weather, bundle it up for the winter with a mulch, or wrap the branches in burlap and stuff leaves or excelsior inside. This treatment can stretch your plant choices through the next zone or two north. If you want to grow a plant that needs cold, leave the winter mulch off the plant and keep the soil on the dry side, so as much cold as possible can penetrate the soil. A small burlap sunscreen on the south side of the plant would help, too. Or grow the plant on the north side of a structure where it gets shade in the winter and the proper amount of sun in the summer.

You can create a micro-climate on the south side of your home or in a protected niche created by abutting walls of your house. Winter-tender roots planted close to the wall of a heated basement will often survive—the top can survive if covered with a rose cone or heavy box filled with leaves or excelsior.

Experimenting with tender plants may be a little expensive, but an occasional venture may result in your having a plant no one else in the area has, with the feeling of accomplishment that goes with it.

INDEX